SELLING THE CLOUD

A PLAYBOOK FOR SUCCESS IN CLOUD SOFTWARE AND ENTERPRISE SALES

BY MARK PETRUZZI AND PAUL MELCHIORRE

To our families, the absolute loves of our lives and the reason we have worked so hard every step of the way.

"Thought-provoking, insightful, and just a well-done book that is not only a great sales book but so much more. I highly recommend it to anyone focused on Sales, Customer Success, Channels/Alliances, or any other area where you are responsible for serving a complex B2B client and prospect base." –Ted Malley, Chairman and CEO, Think-X; former CRO and CCO at Ceridian; former Head of Customer Success and CIO, Ultimate Software

"Selling the Cloud is a must read, must share book for anyone interested in building a high powered professional sales team. Mark and Paul debunk the myths about what it takes to be successful in professional sales and provide a useful guide to help you along the way." –Myron Radio, Five-Time Award Winning Author; President of The R Group

"Selling the Cloud is a most welcome book as organizations are learning how to successfully and sustainably pivot to the cloud after the impact of the Covid-19 pandemic. Notably, and because digital sales transformation and shift is primarily driven by strong leadership skills, the book assembles important cloud titans' perspectives on the matter. But the technology and sales stack strategy is not left behind, and it is nice to see how the book also echoes my work on why digital sales transformation is about making technology focus on the process, so you can focus on the customer. Mark and Paul's book is more than just about the 'why' and 'how' of Selling the Cloud, as it is incredibly timely and about the 'when', which is now!" –Joël Le Bon, PhD, Marketing & Sales Professor and Executive Director of The Science of Digital Business Development Initiative, Johns Hopkins University Carey Business School

CONTENTS:

ABOUT MARK PETRUZZI

Mark Petruzzi has worked in the enterprise software and cloud software ecosystem for 25 years. Today he is an industry leader with a distinct focus on channel and alliance program development and execution.

He started his career at The MAC Group, a Harvard-based strategy consulting firm, and has held senior leadership positions at Oracle Consulting, Deloitte Consulting, and HCL, driving exceptional growth and consistently delivering over-target revenue performance. As one of the youngest individuals to ever serve as the director of business development at Deloitte, Mark was instrumental in building both the Oracle and Ariba practices into the largest "Big Four" practice in their respective markets.

Throughout his career, Mark has always been an innovator. He has worked as a serial entrepreneur, founding, growing, and successfully exiting boutique consulting firms in the Salesforce, Oracle, and Peoplesoft ecosystems. He was also an early and key participant in the development of cloud computing, leading one of the first Oracle On Demand initiatives at Oracle Consulting in the late 1990s. This effort launched his career as a leader in channel and alliance sales within the Salesforce ecosystem.

More recently, Mark turned his focus toward developing and executing innovative channel-and-alliance-based go-to-market strategies for cloud software and consulting organizations and general sales and marketing digital transformation. This work includes a unique private equity go-to-market model that he has built for multiple cloud software and services firms.

Committed to philanthropy, Mark has supported children with illnesses, prematurity, and hunger throughout the world through the March of Dimes and UNICEF. He has also supported his children, Max and Mirabella in their personal pursuits launching the charities, Mirabella's Miracle and Flower Power, which are focused on supporting the patients, families, and the incredible front-line medical workers that serve them.

Mark holds a Bachelor of Science degree in Accounting and Philosophy from Rutgers College within Rutgers University, and a Master of Business Administration in Finance and Marketing from Columbia Business School. Additionally, he served as Adjunct Faculty Educator for Duke University CE and NYIT for the sales, marketing and business strategy departments. He lives with his wife, Michelle, and two children, Max and Mirabella in Charlotte, North Carolina.

ABOUT PAUL MELCHIORRE

Paul has 30 years of experience in enterprise software sales and business leadership. Raised in South Philadelphia, Paul is a natural-born salesman and entrepreneur. He started his first business at 13 years old selling newspapers on the beaches of Wildwood, New Jersey. Paul's street smarts and entrepreneurial spirit translated to industry-leading performance in enterprise software sales. His innate ability to identify potential, build company portfolios, and take companies public has rewarded him with an illustrious track record of successful exits.

Paul's passion lies in technology, sales leadership, and building go-to-market strategies. He has applied that passion over his career to influence the enterprise software sales industry. He began his career in the enterprise software space at SAP in its early stages. He joined SAP as employee number 200 in the USA, assisting in the early global deployments of SAP R3. As Senior Vice President of Global accounts, he and his group were responsible for over 85% of the company's revenue and helped establish SAP as the global leader in enterprise software. Paul also led industry initiatives supporting SAP's vertical strategy that enabled it to dominate many industries on a global basis.

Recognizing a void in the market for procurement software, Paul helped found Ariba in 1998 and built the field organization for sales, implementation, service, alliances, and channels. Ariba was eventually acquired by SAP for $5 billion in 2012. Paul went on to help several other Software as a Service (SaaS) portfolio companies go public.

Recently, he served as President and Chief Revenue Officer at Anaplan, a leading SaaS platform to facilitate financial planning and management. There, he contributed to a successful IPO in 2018, and saw the company grow from $80 million to $300+ million in annual recurring revenue and to over a $7 billion market cap.

Paul is now sharing his proven, innovative approach as Operating Partner at Stripes. He also serves as an independent director at both R3, an enterprise blockchain technology company, and Scout RFP, a sourcing and procurement software company that was acquired in December 2019 by Workday, as well as nonprofit Spark.org.

Dedicated to giving back, Paul's philanthropic efforts have advanced education for children, future mental health professionals, and women's heart health, through Spark, The Quell Foundation, and The American Heart Association.

Paul holds a Bachelor of Science in Marketing from Villanova University and a Master of Business Administration in Finance from Drexel University. He and his wife, Nicole, have four children and reside in Philadelphia, PA.

Amateurs score occasional wins. Professionals create consistent results. Top sales professionals don't make quota, they exceed quota. They don't make sales, they create customers. They don't dream of earning a good living, they are living the good life.

This book captures the time-tested sales wisdom of great salespeople that realized early in their career that learning means earning. I have had the privilege of interviewing some of the best salespeople in the world, from Europe and Japan to the United States, and learned that all great salespeople consciously develop five qualities that all begin with the letter "C".

Curiosity: Great salespeople are curious about people, processes, financial matters and customer psychology.

Creativity: When Bill McDermott, the CEO of ServiceNow worked as a Xerox salesman, he made a sales call with a colleague in New York City. They visited an elderly woman who was interested in buying a copy machine. As they entered the room, Bill was attacked by her cat. In a flash, he realized that the owner loves the cat and he was curious about the owner's fondness for cats. Bill realized that currying favor with the cat was the way to the sale. It worked. They sold the copy machine without talking about the product and without giving a product demonstration.

Credibility: Dr. Robert Cialdini, a leading expert on persuasion shared a story about a real estate company: When customers called to get more information, the receptionist was trained to say, "I'll connect you with Peter, the head of sales. He has over 20 years of experience selling high-end properties..." That credibility statement resulted in 20% more appointments and 15% more sales. Great salespeople turn credibility into success.

Communication: Great salespeople know how to share a compelling story at the right moment. They know how to break the ice with a humble, self-deprecating comment. But they also know how to listen, and they allow their customers to express themselves fully, frankly, and freely.

Courage: It takes internal fortitude to call on CEO's or C-level executives and present a well thought out solution in a compelling way, without glossing over the drawbacks and potential risks. It takes courage to speak the truth. It takes courage to do the right thing. It takes courage to right a wrong and it takes courage to stand up for what you believe in.

This book contains many gems that highlight these qualities, gathered and polished by today's sales top sales titans. Read on to learn how to dazzle in your sales career.

#1 | PASSION & MINDSET

DETERMINATION AND DRIVE WILL SET YOU APART

"Working hard for something we don't care about is called stress; working hard for something we love is called passion."

– Simon Sinek

Most people do not grow up dreaming that they will one day work in sales. In fact, "sales" is a deterrent word for many. People shy away from the career path because they correlate it with smarmy used car salesmen, impersonal spam emails, and unsolicited phone calls. But the sales stereotypes of yesterday are evolving. Rather than being associated with disingenuous tactics, sales is increasingly associated with drive, determination, and high emotional intelligence levels. Success in sales requires a certain level of natural inclination, resilience, and—perhaps most importantly—passion.

Throughout this book, you will hear stories from Mark and Paul's seasoned experience in sales and business. The lessons in these stories clearly impart the importance of passion and emotional intelligence in sales. Not only that, you will hear lessons from colleagues and friends they grew up with in cloud software sales. Those friends just happen to be some of the most successful and respected technology leaders on the planet, from companies like Salesforce, Microsoft, Cisco, Oracle, Zoom, SAP, and DocuSign. A common thread you will see among them is their focus on doing what is right for the people they serve and maintaining the passion to continue innovating along the way.

The powerful thing about passion is that it is contagious. Our customers can sense when we are not genuinely excited about what we are selling. If you want your prospects to be enthusiastic about what you offer, you need to authentically believe in the solution you provide. Otherwise, your customers will see right through you. The modern customer is savvy. They have more information at their fingertips than ever before. They do not need a list of bullet points telling them why your solution is better; they need an advisor dedicated to helping them fit the solution to their needs. This requires more nuance and passion on our part as salespeople.

The future demands salespeople who are resilient, passionate, and genuinely invested in serving their customers. The enterprise software sales organizations that will thrive in the future will not be bare-minimum organizations. They will be those who develop and nurture a genuine passion for serving their customers and offering an excellent solution—such as the organizations our sales titans, featured throughout this book, lead.

So, how do you develop, embrace, and nurture a passion for sales?

KEEP THE SPARK ALIVE

Cloud software sales is a wonderful way to live a great life and make a great living. Especially now, in our post-COVID-19 world. People embrace technology more readily than ever before, and stocks of successful cloud software companies like Salesforce, Workday and Adobe are trading for 11-18 times revenue. That's revenue, not earnings.

We were taught in business school that stocks should trade at 11-18 earnings, not revenue, but the ticker doesn't lie. Opportunity for financial gains in this industry have never been higher. Valuations are high and plenty of opportunity awaits. But, success does not come without great effort. Even the most talented sales people hear "no" more often than they hear "yes." The work it takes to thrive in sales can be likened to what it takes to maintain a flourishing marriage: a positive mindset, commitment, an ability to learn from adversity, and the ability to be flexible.

The importance of keeping the spark alive doesn't stop with your relationship with your sales career. It also applies to keeping the fire burning in your relationships with prospects and colleagues. Sales gives us the wonderful gift of a network of lasting relationships. It also gives us the opportunity to help our customers and colleagues succeed.

No matter how high the stakes are, our business is not about money; it is about people. Our profession is listening, learning, and positioning our solutions in a way that benefits the people we serve. Remember, the customer is not the company, it is the individual person you are serving. Individuals often stay in the same industry but work for different companies over their careers. You never know when you might have the opportunity to work with a former prospect, customer, or colleague again. That is why it is incredibly important to keep relationships positive and to continually check your network to learn how to better serve customers, colleagues, and competitors alike.

OWN YOUR MINDSET

"The view you adopt for yourself profoundly affects the way you lead your life."

- Satya Nadella, CEO of Microsoft

Lighting the fire for your prospects starts with lighting the fire within yourself. When is the last time you set aside time to think about what you do and why you do it? Ask yourself:

- Do I enjoy my profession?
- Why do I do what I do?

If you never take the time to think about what you do and why it brings you joy, burnout is inevitable, and your relationships and quotas will suffer along with your mental health. You will spend over 1/3 of your life working, so make it something you are passionate about doing. Not to mention that if you find passion in what you do, you are much more likely to succeed in the profession, especially in a profession like sales that consistently knocks you down. Keep your mindset positive and focus on what brings you joy in your work.

When challenges come up in sales, it is common to feel defeated and try to sidestep the hurdle. However, you have another option. You can immerse yourself in the challenge and learn something new. The latter approach typically helps you earn respect among your colleagues and customers, contributes to a better bottom line, and helps you develop a deeper and fuller sense of purpose. The ability to thrive through adversity is what separates the most successful from the least successful.

The future of enterprise software sales has a growth mindset. This means believing that your most basic abilities can evolve through dedication and hard work. In other words, book smarts and natural talent are just the tip of the iceberg. The true differentiator is being willing to lean in, learn, and overcome adversity.

EMBRACE THE SKIN-IN-THE-GAME NATURE OF THE WORK

To some, a sales quota is as anxiety inducing as a final exam. To those with a passion for sales, we don't think a whole lot about the quota. We focus on doing the right things for the right reasons—crushing the quota is an added benefit. We are not deterred by the fact that we have skin-in-the-game. Instead, it is invigorating and inspiring. In sales, we have the unique opportunity to be connected with the public-facing and internal-facing aspects of the company we serve. This gives us the power to make an impact far beyond our sales totals. A thoughtful and passionate salesperson does a lot more than sell; they bring innovative ideas back to leadership and operations based on the feedback received from prospects and current customers and have the power to help shape the evolution of a company.

GET COMFORTABLE LIVING WITHOUT LIMITS

Sales is not just a job. Those who want to clock in and clock out at a nine-to-five job need not apply. Sales is a lifestyle. This does not mean you must be chained to your iPhone or desk all day every day. However, it does require you to be available outside of business hours. The tradeoff for that sacrifice is the opportunity to live more freely than your contemporaries with desk jobs.

As a salesperson, you are in control of your own destiny. Whether you sell $10,000 or $10,000,000 a month, you have not reached your limit—only your limit to-date. You own your own productivity and efficiency levels, and it falls to you to ensure you are doing the right things for the right reasons to move the needle. If you get out of sync working too much or start focusing on the wrong accounts because you are struggling or trying to build your pipeline, you will flounder. If you hone your craft and optimize how you spend your time, you will soar.

The limitless nature of sales does not stop with income level and work hours, it also applies to the scope of your network. In sales, you will not go into the same office every day and see the same 30–40 people. You will travel the country and world and meet many people from a variety of backgrounds. As a salesperson—especially in enterprise software sales—you have the opportunity to visit and interact with people from countless countries and learn about different cultures.

THRIVE ON THE OPPORTUNITY TO CONSTANTLY LEARN AND GROW

When people do not feel challenged in their careers, they lose drive. Fortunately, in sales, you are pushed to evolve every day. Change is constant and is only becoming more constant. We love sales because it consistently keeps us on our toes. If frequent change and fast-paced pivots aren't for you, sales may not be for you.

For example, when Paul started a new job at SAP, a German company starting up operations in the U.S., he learned that the model for sales in the U.S. was quite different than the model in Germany. Paul was accustomed to having pre-sales support and support from colleagues on the technical architecture side. In Germany, the sales reps didn't need that support because they could code and demo the software themselves. The German team referred to the U.S.-based sales team as "Türgriffpolierer" or "doorknob polishers." Paul learned very quickly that what he had learned as a salesperson over the first decade of his career was not going to work at SAP. He embraced this opportunity to grow. He took a training class with the consultant team on coding. It was as far out of his comfort zone as he could imagine. But, because he invested in learning what he needed to learn to be successful, he rose through the ranks and became the top sales rep within two years. Paul learned SAP's product so well that many of his German colleagues thought he was a product architect.

Mark had a similar experience at Deloitte. At 29 years old, he was told he was the youngest individual yet to be offered a Director of Business Development role. He quickly learned why most other business development leaders in his practice area were 20+ years his senior. It was the power of their networks. Knowing how important relationships are to sales success, Mark was intimidated by his senior colleagues' full rolodexes.

He had two choices, find a new job, or improvise and adapt. After a couple of weeks of frustration, he had an epiphany. He realized that despite his smaller C-Suite network, he had a larger network of enterprise software sales leaders like Paul. Someone like Paul who is plugged into a large software ecosystem could connect Mark to 10 deals at once, while an old friend who is a CEO may only be tied to one deal.

So, Mark leaned into the enterprise software sales partnership-style selling. He learned that not only did it connect him to more deals, faster, those deals had the potential to grow exponentially. As long as his team delivered great work, they were introduced to more deals within the enterprise ecosystem.

SELL LIKE YOU

If what you do every day is not in line with who you are, your performance will suffer. You may think you need to sell in a certain way or like a certain person, but we know that the best salespeople have a style all their own. In the sales market of the future, those who tune into their own sense of humor, creativity, and charisma will rise to the top of the pack.

Many aspiring salesmen read every single "how-to" sales book and think they can make people do things they do not want to do. However, no book is a better reference point than your gut feeling—if it feels like the right thing to do, it probably is the right thing to do. There are strategies that can help you optimize your efforts, but, at a basic level, the main thing you need to do is authentically support your clients.

When you fight against your own intrinsic nature, failure is inevitable. You will feel like a phony and your prospects and colleagues will sense the phoniness too. If you are not enjoying what you're doing or believing what you're saying, no one else with either.

The antidote to phoniness and—dare we say it—desperation is going back to basics. Ask yourself:

- Do I know what is most important to every prospect in my pipeline?
- How can I help find a solution that drives what is most important to them?

We thrive when we are in tune with our intrinsic nature and flounder when we are out of balance. If your intentions are pure, chances are you are in tune with your intrinsic nature and your career will be more successful and rewarding.

CHAPTER TAKEAWAYS

You need passion to thrive in sales because you will hear "no" more often than "yes."

TIPS FOR NURTURING YOUR SALES PASSION:

- Know your why. Ask yourself, why do I do what I do?

- Focus on helping customers, not selling them.

- Keep in touch with past colleagues and clients.

Stay mentally strong because your mindset will drive your sales success or failure.

TIPS FOR A STRONG MINDSET:

- Surround yourself with mentally strong people.

- Don't focus on your sales quota, focus on doing the right things for the right reasons every day.

- View adversity as a learning opportunity.

Be yourself. Your prospects, colleagues, and customers will see through inauthenticity.

TIPS FOR SELLING LIKE YOU:

- Be vulnerable with prospects.

- Think about what success means to you.

- Set goals that reflect your version of a successful day.

CLOUD TITAN:
GERHARD GSCHWANDTNER,
FOUNDER AND CEO OF
SELLING POWER INC.

How your Mindset leads to successful customer relationships

Gerhard is the Founder and CEO of Selling Power, Inc., a media company that produces Selling Power magazine, the number one industry resource for sales management executives. Over the course of three decades, he has interviewed some of the most successful leaders and experts in sales, business, sports, entertainment, and politics, including Mary Kay Ash, Marc Benioff, Michael Dell, Seth Godin, Jay Leno, Bill Marriott, Dr. Norman Vincent Peale, Meg Whitman, Richard Branson and Colin Powell. He's trained more than 10,000 salespeople around the world and is the author of 17 sales management books.

Everyone talks about customer relationships. But what is a relationship? It describes a vital connection between people.

Let's break the word into two parts. There is the word relation and then there is the word ship. A ship transports people from one part of the world to another. The ship makes the connection. We sometimes say, "we're all in the same boat," suggesting that we have something in common. Customer relationships are about how we make connections with our customers. What connects us is that the customer has the need, and we have the solution. To sell, we have to navigate through corporate channels, we get the order and then ship the product to the customer. That's where most relationships slow down and fade out.

WHAT GOVERNS YOUR CUSTOMER RELATIONSHIPS?

You may not be aware of this truth: the relationship you have with yourself is the blueprint that governs your relationship with others. When sales leaders coach salespeople and try to help them create better customer relationships, they focus on the how-to, or on the what to. What they often fail to explore is the salesperson's belief system. W. Clement Stone once said, what the mind can conceive and believe it can achieve. If a salesperson believes that he or she is not good enough to call on C-level executives, then they will do everything they can to avoid that challenge. They know how to dial, they know who to contact, they know how to ask questions and how to listen. But they won't do any of this if they believe that they are not good enough. Self-doubt kills more opportunities than any economic downturn.

NEGATIVE SELF-TALK IS THE BIGGEST BARRIER TO SUCCESS

Research by NIH revealed that we experience over 60,000 thoughts a day. What's surprising is that 80% of these thoughts are negative.

Psychologists found that in order to flourish, we need a ratio of 3:1 between positive and negative thoughts. This means that if you are not consciously working on creating more positive thoughts in your mind, you are not likely to reach your goals.

Dr. Martin Seligman, the author of the book Learned Optimism discovered that salespeople with little aptitude for selling, but with optimistic explanatory styles would (after receiving skills training) outsell salespeople that had a high aptitude for sales, but habitually explained what was happening in their world in a negative narrative.

HOW DO YOU SHIFT FROM NEGATIVE SELF-TALK TO A POSITIVE MINDSET?

The best way for changing your Mindset is to go through a four-step mindfulness exercise. First, awareness, second acceptance, third understanding, fourth, conscious change.

You gain awareness of your thoughts by sitting quiet for five minutes and observing your thoughts without judging them. Imagine that you are the owner of a guest house and assume that each thought is a guest that enters your home. You become aware that thoughts come and go. Your role is not to judge your thoughts or engage them in a confrontative way. Trying to fight your negative thoughts will make you feel worse.

Accept your thoughts. Imagine that you are sitting in your favorite chair in your house and a negative thought enters your living room.

Accept its presence, observe the thought, and become aware of its curious nature. It's just another thought passing through.

The more you observe your thoughts, you become aware that you are NOT your thoughts. You can shift your mind into observation mode. You are mildly curious. You accept what is. Once you accept the thought and recognize its fragile nature you begin to understand that thoughts are not real and that every thought will transform the closer you observe it – without fighting it.

While you observe your thoughts, you can shift your focus on your breathing. As you inhale you can say, "I am aware of my body," and as you exhale you say, "I am letting go of all my tensions."

After four or five breaths you will notice a change in your physiology and your psychology. You will feel more relaxed and in charge of your own mind and you may wonder why the negative thoughts have vanished.

SELLING IS A TRANSFER OF ENERGY

Have you ever wondered why some conversations with customers leave you energized, while others leave you feeling drained? Great salespeople know how to prepare for a sales call by shifting into a state of positive energy. There are two ways to create a peak performance state of mind. One way to increase your energy and confidence is to stand up, lift your arms above your head and assume the victory position. Imagine you just ran a marathon and won first place. Hold the position for two minutes. You'll notice how your mind shifted from negative to positive, any feelings of self-doubt have vanished, and you are feeling confident and ready to take on the world.

Another way to achieve a high-performance state is to remind yourself of your "why". Why are you in sales? Why are you calling on this customer? Are you in sales for the money? For the thrill of the hunt? For the opportunity to win? For creating a family, for providing for your children, for buying a vacation home, for contributing to a better world? Remember, the bigger the why, the bigger the try and the easier the how.

ALL SUCCESS BEGINS WITH YOUR MINDSET

Sales success depends on three factors: the right Mindset, the right skillset and the best tool set. It all begins with the Mindset. The mindset is like the operating system of a computer that needs to be upgraded periodically in order to function at full capacity.

Neuroscience tells us that the prefrontal cortex is where your "Inner CEO" is located. It is your inner CEO that's in control of your Mindset operating system. If you were to study a brain scan of an average salesperson or sales leader, you'd see that certain regions of the brain are not fully activated when they are interacting with their customers. Their minds often run in "automatic" mode. Automatic mode means limited awareness and lack of focus.

They are unaware that it is their negative self-commentary (while they interact with others) that is inhibiting their capacity to handle difficult situations at work.

This limited awareness reduces their ability to advise customers on the best course of action.

They don't know how to improve their Mindsets to achieve better results.

They are so caught up in their daily routine and tethered to their habits that they forget that they are human beings, not human doings.

They ignore their mental states and ignore the fact that happy salespeople sell 38% more.

They are not aware that people with a positive Mindset live on average 7.5 years longer.

They are unaware that their self-limiting beliefs stand in the way of them reaching their goals.

They are unaware that their minds get distracted by their three internal time zones: the past, the present and the future. It's like watching the History Channel, CNN and a SciFi channel all at once.

Unsuccessful people spend too much of their time ruminating about their negative past which causes them to give up on their dreams.

They don't have their goals in writing and they never bother to explore their "why?

They don't see the connection between their poor diet and lack of exercise and their low energy levels.

They don't know why top performing leaders seek solutions while they average performers seek comfort.

The Mindset of the herd is to do what comes easy. The Mindset of the peak performer is to do what's hard.

#2 | VELOCITY & GRIT

HARD WORK DIVIDES "GET BY" SALESPEOPLE FROM THOSE WHO THRIVE.

"Selling is the easiest job in the world if you work it hard, but the hardest job in the world if you try to work it easy"

- Fred Bettger author of How I Raised Myself from Failure

As we discussed in chapter 1, passion for the profession is critical to building a successful career in enterprise-level software sales and consulting in the hyper growth market. As the market evolves, the emotional intelligence and ability to connect with your customers will become increasingly important and any lack of passion will come through as apathy. Functioning as a dispassionate salesperson will not only drain you mentally and emotionally, but will also repel customers. However, passion alone will not keep your career afloat, just as passion alone does not sustain a marriage. Feeling a spark for sales might land you the job or get you the meeting, but a solid commitment to the grind (what we'll refer to as "velocity and grit" in this chapter) is what will help your career sustainably grow.

Everyone understands velocity and we all work to achieve it. But, what is grit? Grit, as defined by the Merriam-Webster dictionary, is "a firmness of mind or spirit: unyielding courage in the face of hardship or danger."

Margaret M. Perlis' 2013 Forbes article "5 Characteristics of Grit —How Many do you Have?" defines grit as:

1. Courage

2. Conscientiousness: achievement-oriented versus dependable

3. Long-term goals and endurance: follow through

4. Resilience: optimism, confidence, and creativity

5. Excellence versus perfection

This is really it. If you have the above, you are well along the way to a successful sales career. There is more, which is why we have written this book, but grit is so important to us that we cover it throughout the book. If there is one word that describes the skills necessary to sales success, it is grit.

In addition to grit, sustainable sales success requires steady action, work, and an unending dedication to the process. We have more ability to connect, collaborate, and create than ever before in the history of the world. Because of this, we believe those who are willing to consistently take action to maintain the velocity and grit to keep going when challenging times arise have the opportunity to actualize the most fulfilling and prolific sales careers to have existed.

When you think of velocity and grit, consider the fact that your relationship with your prospects, your colleagues, and your customers will not remain strong without tending. The relationships that make up the very fiber of your success do not sprout, grow, and thrive in any condition. They cannot be neglected, and they require thoughtful and consistent care and attention. Because of this, only the most dedicated and nurturing salespeople will grow the sturdiest and most fruitful relationships over time.

Being a dedicated and nurturing salesperson requires building a process you trust and showing up consistently to execute it. When you have a reliable process, you are freed from the looming pressure of sales targets and quotas. Ironically, velocity and grit do not necessarily require working more or working harder—they require working smarter and more methodically.

HAVE AN EXCELLENT PROCESS, NOT A PLAYBOOK

The reality is sales is hard work; world-class salespeople stand apart from "get-by" salespeople because they have a tried and tested process. We believe in processes. However, we also believe that companies spend more time and money than they should on promoting specific sales methodologies. There are countless sales books that promise to share the "secret sauce" to make your sales results soar, but most sales methodologies are basically the same. Similar to implementation methodologies for software, there are many methodology versions, but they all boil down to common pillars. When it comes down to it, it is not the methodologies that drive success. Instead, it is good leadership, a consistent process, and the intuition of hardworking human beings.

In our experience, the most critical part of the sales process is the discovery process. As sales author Elmer Wheeler said, "Your first ten words are more important than your next ten thousand." Many sales are won and lost during the discovery stage. If you cannot understand your customer's issues and pain points and match what you have to offer to their needs, you will not be able to differentiate your product and service in a meaningful way. The buyer of the future has more options than ever. Therefore, it's easier than ever to disqualify yourself early on in the sales process.

Perfecting your discovery process does not only help you win sales; it helps you avoid pursuing sales that are not a good fit. Working with a prospect through the sales process is time and resource intensive, and it is not worthwhile to pursue a deal that is not a good fit for your solution. This is another reason why it is so vital to have a healthy pipeline. When you have a pipeline of solid opportunities, you can confidently disqualify opportunities that are not good fits early on in the process.

"Write down a plan, execute that plan, and measure yourself against the plan. Over time, every idea gets copied, but execution is enduring. Spend 90%+ on execution."
- Peter Gassner, Founder & CEO, Veeva Systems

PRIORITIZE YOUR PIPELINE, IT'S YOUR LIFEBLOOD

We all know the importance of pipeline development. Nothing happens unless you're filling your funnel. Companies in our industry have struggled with this for years. Even the most successful continue to have difficulties in a few key areas. Do any of these following statements sound familiar?

"We have spent tens or sometimes hundreds of millions of dollars on building up the facilities and talent to try to build up an effective internal Business Development Representative (BDR) capability. Why are we not getting a reasonable return on investment?"

"Why do we keep spending more in outbound marketing and keep generating the same amount or less leads?"

"Why does our cost of sales keep increasing and our performance per rep keep decreasing?"

"Why do we keep hiring expensive outside sales reps with what appear to be significant networks that just never pay off?"

"Why does Marketing always blame Sales and vice versa?"

"Why does every lead generation and appointment scheduling service over promise and under deliver, especially the ones who try to deliver the capability from an offshore location to the market being targeted?"

Very simply, the work of filling your pipeline is not easy and very few companies excel at it, even those that specialize in delivering outsourced lead generation and inside sales. However, it is crucial to develop prospecting skills whether you are a sales rep or a sales leader.

If you're a direct sales rep, learn this skill early and invest your time wisely to ensure prospecting is a core competency of yours. If you can always successfully build a pipeline, you will always be valuable. Sales leaders will help you reel in a deal, but you are responsible for building a healthy pipeline of prospects.

So, what drives a healthy pipeline? You guessed it: a healthy process. As we discussed in the previous section, we are advocates for processes, not playbooks. We believe all sales training programs are limited. There are no quick-fix sales hacks that will keep your pipeline flowing like a well-oiled machine. A dedicated person who is willing to define and hold themselves accountable to a process and change portions of that process that aren't working will have a happy pipeline. In other words, success is driven by your work ethic and creativity, not checking off boxes in a sales manual.

A well-defined process starts with well-defined goals and clear intentions. Ask yourself:

- Do you have a process you follow to pursue outbound leads?

- Where do you find your best prospects?

- When you find them, how do you engage them?

- When you're engaging with them, do you define a purpose for your conversation and a planned next step?

- Do you have a solid set of discovery questions you ask your prospects?

- Once you are sure you can help your prospects, do you know how you will follow up?

When is the last time you worked backwards from your goals and made a roadmap to determine how you can realistically get there? What are you doing every day to ensure you're taking a step toward your goals? If you don't have clear intentions and goals, it's very difficult (if not impossible) to make a plan, prioritize the way you spend your energy, and make strides every day toward achieving your goals. When you take the time to look at the big picture, you are more likely to ask for the next logical commitments rather than leaving next steps undefined.

DON'T FILL YOUR PIPELINE WITH BLIND RFPS

When it comes to pipeline building, focus on quality over quantity. A full pipeline is worthless if it isn't filled with quality opportunities. Here is a story that illustrates our point:

Melissa is a senior business developer. She is well known in her firm for consistently having a small pipeline yet exceeding her quota year after year. It seems counterintuitive. Isn't a larger pipeline more likely to deliver higher year-end numbers? Not necessarily.

Melissa's explanation for her unique success is simple. She does not bid on blind Requests for Proposals (RFPs). She knows that pursuing a lead is a significant investment of time and resources. To that end, she analyzes every potential lead to determine if she should invest the firm's resources to chase it. Since she spends so much time determining which deals to pursue, she has a much smaller total pipeline than her peers. However, her close ratio is much higher.

By taking the time to analyze each lead and turn away opportunities that are not good fits, she earns the respect of both her clients and prospects. She does this by not only being forthcoming when she doesn't believe her firm is a good fit, but also recommending a better fitting firm.

Ultimately, if Melissa determines that her firm would not truly shine doing the work, she passes on the short-term benefit of signing another deal. Instead, she pursues the long-term gains of delivering outstanding work to her clients and building up the firm's reputation over time. In the short term, this approach is not always well received by internal team members. Melissa often has to fight the internal battle all the way up to the executive offices. But she is prepared because her results speak for themselves.

You may think the Melissas of the world are naïve, moralists, or do-gooders. But this Melissa not only beats quota consistently—she has the respect and admiration of her clients, her peers, and her management.

PREPARE. PREPARE. PREPARE.

In baseball, you get three strikes. In sales, you get one. As we mentioned earlier in this chapter, most sales are won and lost during the discovery process. That is exactly why preparing for your sales meetings will set you apart. Preparing may seem like the price of admission to a sales career, but we are consistently blown away by how few salespeople do it. Performing research ahead of time, preparing an agenda, and coming to the table with thoughtful questions will set you apart from the pack.

When you enter a meeting prepared and demonstrate expertise out of the gate, you establish immediate credibility. Being prepared doesn't mean writing a script and sticking to it. It means walking into a meeting knowing a little something about your prospect or client's background, having a list of questions that will help you find out how your solution might benefit them, and a next step to continue the conversation. Ideally, you have an idea of where your conversation will go, but you are flexible enough to listen intently and pivot when you uncover a different need.

When preparing for a call, ensure you know a little bit about your contact's background. Try to find answers to these questions:

1. Where do they come from?
2. What are they more driven by: logic or emotion?
3. How might purchasing your solution affect their job and/or their team?

Knowing the answers to these questions will help you adjust your approach to their personality and tailor your message to their motivations. For example, if you are working with an analytical buyer, they likely won't want to spend much time on small talk. On the other hand, with a more emotional buyer who likes to chat, you will scare them off with an immediate spreadsheet. You need to be flexible enough to play all four quadrants of the personality chart.

The last thing you want to do is ask a question you could answer with basic research. There are so many sources of information available to you—Google, LinkedIn, public annual reports, Crunchbase, chatting with your contact's administrative assistant. You have one shot at making a first impression with a prospect, and you never know what piece of information or insider knowledge will help set you apart.

"Everything is accelerating in this world. There's more information than ever and salespeople are no longer the providers of information. They need to transform into providers of insight. If they're not able to do that quickly, they'll waste a lot of time. They need to have very clear and simple messages for the buyer in order to engage them on an emotional level that generates interest. Salespeople need to change the conversation from pitching to co-creating value with the customer or for the customer."

- Gerhard Gschwandtner, Founder and CEO of Selling Power

In addition to doing your research, an important part of preparation is knowing your intention. Make sure you know the goal of your meeting. Maybe it is to find out the name of the decision maker. Maybe it is to get the next meeting on the calendar. Or, perhaps your goal is to have the prospect ask for a proposal or quote. Whatever it is, most of your sales calls won't include closing the sale during the call. Get comfortable setting different goals that support the buyer's journey along the way.

Once you have done your research and set your intention, there is one last important part of preparation—getting your mind right. It is important that you are in a good headspace to make your call. Take a deep breath. Imagine yourself in a calm and positive state. This quote from Brian Tracy puts it well:

"Stop for a few seconds and create a clear mental picture of yourself as completely relaxed, calm, positive, smiling, and in complete control of the interview. Then inhale deeply, filling up your lungs and putting pressure on your diaphragm. Hold this breath for a count of seven and exhale for a count of seven. While you are breathing deeply, continue to hold a picture of yourself as the very best salesperson you could possibly be."

- Brian Tracy, Author of The Psychology of Selling: Increase your Sales Faster than You Ever Thought Possible

ALWAYS KEEP EVOLVING

"Keep in mind that the landscape is always changing; you must always examine what's working, evolve your ideas, and change the way you do things."

- Marc Benioff, Behind the Cloud: The Untold Story of How salesforce.com Went from Idea to Billion-Dollar Company-and Revolutionized an Industry

Part of the velocity and grit that it takes to succeed in sales—especially the hypergrowth sales world of tomorrow—includes getting comfortable with an endlessly accelerating pace of change. We must learn through our own research and through living the highs and lows of the sales lifestyle every day. The agony of defeat and the thrill of a win are both excellent teachers. Success requires learning from wins and losses. In other words, to succeed you must evolve.

Most thriving salespeople have a regular practice of seeking out new knowledge on the latest insights in the profession. This may be by listening to audio recordings, reading a book, or attending workshops and motivational seminars. At a base level, successful salespeople intuitively know that they need to constantly grow to become more adept at building lasting relationships and to keep up with the way modern customers buy.

CHAPTER TAKEAWAYS

TRUE COMMITMENT WILL DRIVE THE SUSTAINABILITY OF YOUR CAREER

Those who are willing to invest time and energy into their sales process have the opportunity to actualize the most fulfilling and prolific sales careers to have ever existed.

TIPS FOR NURTURING A SUSTAINABLE CAREER:

- Do not neglect your relationships. Keep in touch with prospects, colleagues, past colleagues, and customers.

- Be consistent. Always execute what you say you will, This builds trust.

- Don't be complacent. Always keep evolving by continually seeking out new knowledge through podcasts, books, conversations with mentors, conferences, etc.

FOCUS ON THE PROCESS

World-class salespeople stand apart from "get-by" salespeople because they have a tried and tested process they work and rework to achieve optimal results.

TIPS FOR A MORE EFFECTIVE SALES PROCESS:

- Always be prepared. Do not show up to a sales meeting without knowing your purpose and desired next step.

- Don't rely on a playbook with "tactics." Instead, focus on what drives your sales process forward and commit to showing up every day to push the process forward.

- If you prioritize one part of your process, prioritize the discovery process. Most sales are won or lost in the discovery phase.

KEEP YOUR PIPELINE PRIMED

When you have a healthy pipeline, you can confidently disqualify opportunities that are not good fits early on in the process.

TIPS TO BUILD A HEALTHY PIPELINE:

- Build your process for pursuing outbound leads around your past successes. Pursue the channels you used to find your current best customers.

- Have a solid set of discovery questions that help you identify how your solution can help your prospect.

Always, always, always have a purpose for your conversations and a planned next step at the end of a conversation.

CLOUD TITAN:
JEFF LAUE, CEO OF N3

How Velocity and Grit Drives the Success of Some of the Most-Respected Cloud Initiatives on the Planet

ABOUT JEFF

As Founder and CEO of N3, Jeff Laue sets the course for the company's vision and strategy. N3 ensures revenue impact for some of the most well-known and successful technology companies in the market today. N3 has experienced significant growth over the last 15 years, expanding globally and serves leading Software as a Service (SaaS) and general technology companies. Jeff has more than 30 years' experience in management, business process transformation, and sales and marketing strategy development and implementation. Prior to founding N3, Jeff was a consulting group partner at Computer Science Corporation where he led large global delivery, sales, and strategy teams responsible for nearly a billion dollars of annual revenue. Jeff holds a Bachelor of Science in Business Administration from the University of Alabama and is an Eagle Scout.

Jeff Laue knows very well that successful SaaS selling initiatives are all about velocity and grit. To drive the type of velocity that is necessary for success in SaaS, you need ambition and perseverance. The cornerstone of Jeff's success has been his ambition and his ability to recognize it in others. Ambition for Jeff is about always learning as much as you can, focusing on your goals, and having a single-mindedness around achieving those goals. He believes that ambition is the adrenaline that enables you to overcome all the roadblocks and distractions you are bound to face throughout your career.

As CEO of N3, one of Jeff's greatest challenges is building teams of people with authentic drive. He finds that the most successful team members are focused, driven, and embody "the triple threat": technical acumen, business savvy, and emotional intelligence. Whether you are new to sales or seasoned, everyone can benefit from channeling their very own triple-threat mentality.

Sameness results in stagnation, and, as the saying goes, "activity creates more activity which in turn creates results." Jeff channels this philosophy to teach his teams that when you constantly find ways to lean in harder and learn, you inherently build velocity. And when you build velocity, you build a sustainable sales career. Jeff says anyone—in the right place at the right time—can sell $1 million in a year. But only those with the triple-threat mentality can sell $1 million in a month, repeatedly.

According to Jeff, the way you apply ambition evolves throughout your career. Early on, he suggests focusing on learning and doing.

Be a sponge. Do the grunt work. Get a feel for your personal sales style. Soak up all you can while you're learning on someone else's ticket. The more action you take, the more you will learn.

Mid-career, he suggests honing your leadership and discovery skills. Study the market. Find a mentor (or three). Know your product. Memorize your niche. Remember to listen to your customer; they have all the information. Take a step back from the day-to-day grind and think about why you do what you do, what works and what doesn't, and make thoughtful changes based on what you learn.

Later in your career, he suggests ownership and generosity. It is time to think long term, to mentor, and to pay it forward to those who are just starting out. Jeff believes there is a reason many of us in Cloud Software work past our financial needs. We want to use all of our hard-earned experience and case examples to pay it back by paying it forward.

Jeff knows that in today's sales environment, prospects have information at their fingertips. Salespeople are more like guides than salesmen. Organizations buy when they are ready to buy, often after much consideration and research before ever speaking with a sales representative. People who gravitate towards sales often like to be in the spotlight, but that characteristic is not necessarily key today. True sales leadership is about putting other people and other people's needs in the spotlight. Aspiring leaders don't become leaders if no one wants to follow them, so focus on building trust. In other words, you need to have "followship" to have leadership.

A great example of this is with Marcel Florez, the President of N3. Marcel has been with Jeff and N3 for 14 of its 15 years. Marcel decided to "follow" Jeff because of the personal and professional attributes he saw in Jeff right from the start. Both have benefited immensely from this relationship

First and foremost they have built a family-like relationship and they know they know they can rely on each other at all times. Marcel has had the opportunity to learn from one of the greats and in turn has grown into a SaaS focused sales leader and they together have built an extremely valuable private business entity in N3.And Jeff gets to sleep better at night knowing he has the utmost confidence in the executive leader he has chosen to run his sales organization across the globe.

Jeff also suggests that maintaining velocity requires spending every day making valuable business propositions to your prospects. That means offering something of value to them based on what you have learned by listening to them. Never recite a list of features and benefits. Instead, focus on being authentic and having genuine concern. This requires having an attitude of gratitude and service. These attitudes alone are the essence of the art and science of selling. The best salespeople are able to focus on the client, understand the business need, and get the client thinking about the future.

In Jeff's experience, this is especially important when retaining and growing current clients. We in the SaaS marketplace live in a world where clients are always moving along a continuum from activation to migration. The reality is, if your customer is not actively using your tool and benefiting from it, they are getting closer to migrating every day. This is where true leadership comes into play. It's up to you to be unrelenting about making sure your customer wins. If you are not ambitious and focused, this will be next to impossible to execute.

When you achieve the growth in your career and become a sales leader, and it's time to build your team, focus on hiring ambition. Focus on hiring and inspiring those with the capacity to be actively engaged in your company and its culture.

The best team members are those who respond well to adversity, because adversity is inevitable in sales. Jeff suggests that we all remember that life is a failure proposition. He tells his team members that if you are batting .333 in baseball, it might not feel great to fail twice as much as you succeed, but the reality is you're at the top. It's the same in sales. The key is getting back up again and again and thinking long term, so you build enough pipeline to feel comfortable losing to win.

One aspect of sales that has always helped Jeff engage clients is the art of storytelling. Jeff finds that the strongest executives are strong storytellers. The term "storyteller" may sound bad, but it alludes the idea of creating an authentic, relatable narrative. Consider any leader, from Roosevelt to Elon Musk, their ability to create a compelling narrative drives their success. Prospects want to be led, they want a lighthouse, they need to understand the vision and it is our jobs as salespeople to step up and be that guiding light. It takes creativity to create an effective narrative to excite clients short-term and keep their confidence long-term.

Ambition is not always easy. Over Jeff's career, there were days when it was harder than others to listen, to learn, and to lead. However, Jeff's guiding light has been to always focus on doing the right thing for the right reasons to move the process forward. His motivation as a leader comes from remembering that he does what he does to serve others.

This type of perspective is important for the modern Chief Revenue Officer (CRO). The CRO position often has high turnover because there is so much financial pressure. But the leaders that last are those that consistently keep a laser focus on doing the right things for the right reasons, not a laser focus on earning a higher valuation or just hitting numbers.

No matter how special the "big break" you are offered, it will get you nowhere if you don't bring your own ambition and drive to the opportunity. When you are given a lot, much is expected. The best way to have a great sales career is to open your eyes to the mentors around you and to listen to them and apply their lessons to your work. The more you know, the better you get at betting (i.e., the better you get at choosing the right people and the right opportunities). Over time, Jeff believes that this approach will help you not only survive a career in sales but thrive in it.

TITAN TIPS:

THROW YOUR HEART OVER THE BAR
Don't be afraid to be vulnerable. Take chances, but have a plan. Passionately work the plan. Evaluate the situation and learn from it when your plan fails.

HAVE A PLAN AND WORK IT HARD EVERY DAY
This is where focusing on velocity and being gritty pays you back every day.

THINK WITH YOUR HEART AND FEEL WITH YOUR BRAIN, THE OPPOSITE OF WHAT MOST PEOPLE DO
This might not come naturally to most people in software and technology. But those who embrace this will enjoy success.

#3

EMPATHY

LISTEN TO UNDERSTAND AND SERVE
RATHER THAN PUSH AND SELL

"At the end of the day, we are not selling. We are serving."

- Dave Ramsey, Best Selling Author and Radio Host

The days of telling a customer what you have to offer instead of asking what they need are over. To succeed, we must LISTEN to our customers. This requires leaving our desires at the door and tuning into our customer's true needs. It asks that we advise, not dictate. Serve, not sell.

In order to best serve your customers, you must have a high level of emotional intelligence. Those with a high emotional quotient (EQ) are masters of the art of listening respectfully and actively. This ability is key as you embrace the role of trusted advisor to your prospects. If you don't hear what your customers are telling you in a way that helps you better understand them, where they come from, and where you are going, your efforts will fall flat.

When you have a high level of emotional intelligence, you are able to be vulnerable with your prospects, which builds trust, credibility, and intimacy. Doing so puts you in an incredible position to differentiate your solution.

"Every employee at Workday thinks about how they are going to help customers be successful. It is a simple formula, but a lot of companies go out, and they don't listen to their customers; they don't try to solve hard problems, making it tougher for themselves to create a great business."

- Aneel Bhusri, CEO at Workday

TAPPING INTO YOUR SOFT SIDE

Whether you are selling as a cloud sales rep, an attorney or a bartender, there is a certain baseline ability to listen well and engage others that separates the top sellers from the middle-of-the-road salespeople. That baseline ability is emotional intelligence. For the most part, emotional intelligence is essentially common sense. But it is less common than you might think. People who are emotionally intelligent are likable, enthusiastic, and trustworthy. They are not difficult to be around, irritable, or negative.

If you have a high EQ, you are self-aware, able to build and maintain meaningful connections with other people, empathetic, and enthusiastic. This is important in sales because people buy from people they like. You can have the most logical list of reasons why someone should buy from you, but ultimately your prospect will likely base their decision on your ability to appeal to their emotions. Of course, features and pricing affect purchase decisions, but emotions play a large role. So, the better you understand how your prospect feels, the better chance you have of closing the sale.

People with low levels of emotional intelligence do not handle rejection well and they are not self-motivated, both of which are career-killers in sales (and most other careers for that matter!). Numerous studies have shown that people with high levels of emotional intelligence are more likely to succeed than those with high IQs or relevant experience.[1]

Sellers with high EQs have the patience to maintain enthusiasm through long sales cycles, adapt to their prospects' emotional states, remain positive despite frequent rejection, and build strong bonds with customers that improve retention rates, client satisfaction, and customer success in the long term.

So how can you boost your EQ? Here are a few things to keep in mind:

- Be mindful of your own emotional state.
- Listen more than you speak.
- Spend time putting yourself in your customer's shoes.
- Take responsibility for your own mistakes.
- Don't be afraid to be vulnerable.
- Try to be positive whenever possible.
- Always be curious—ask more questions.
- Get comfortable with adversity.
- Keep stress at bay.

WOMEN IN SALES

As sales has shifted to increasingly favor those with high EQs, we have witnessed more and more women rising through the ranks, often growing to become the most effective sales professionals on the team. In fact, Hubspot reports that women are 5% more likely

---

1. Deutschendorf, Harvey. "Why Emotionally Intelligent People Are More Successful." Fast Company, Fast Company, 22 June 2015, www.fastcompany.com/3047455/why-emotionally-intelligent-people-are-more-successful.

to close a deal than men. This should not be a surprising fact. We believe the higher effectiveness is directly tied to the fact that many women are naturally emotionally intuitive. This characteristic makes women natural fits for sales due to their innate ability to build trust, nurture relationships, and listen.

SALES WORKFORCE[2]

Despite the rise of successful female sales professionals, women only make up about 39% of the sales workforce-- a number that has only grown only by 3% over the past decade--according to a 2018 LinkedIn report. Furthermore, only 19% of VP and C-suite sales positions are held by women. Not to mention, the sales profession has the second-largest gender equity gap in America compared with other professions.

We believe this trend should and will change. The results of diversifying your salesforce speak for themselves. A study by the University of Illinois at Chicago found that companies with higher gender diversity, in general, are 15% more likely to have higher profit. Other research has shown that organizations with women in board member roles have a 42% higher return on sales than companies with fewer female board directors. Not only that, but women stay an average of 1 year longer in their roles than men and a slightly higher percentage of women make their quota over men (70% vs 67%).

VP/C-SUITE POSITIONS HELD BY WOMEN[3]

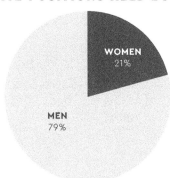

Given this, innovative sales organizations of the future would do well to diversify their salesforce, executive leadership team, and work to rectify gender inequality in the workplace. So 50/50 should be the lowest goal, however from what we have seen in the field, 75% female to 25% might be more your experience if you really hire for the right attributes and capabilities.

2. "The State of Women in Sales." Lucidchart, 2020, www.lucidchart.com/pages/research/women-in-sales.

3. Voria, Rakhi. "Council Post: Why We Need More Women In Sales." Forbes, Forbes Magazine, 17 Jan. 2018, www.forbes.com/sites/forbesbusinessdevelopmentcouncil/2018/01/17/why-we-need-more-women-in-sales/.

LISTEN WISELY

"Sales professionals and marketers, especially in technology start-ups, will talk in depth about the features and functionality without considering what really matters to their customers. You must take a few steps back and look at your product or service positioning from your customer's perspective."

- Dustin Grosse, CMO at DocuSign

If you think your primary task is to sell, think again. Your primary task is to listen and to move the process along in a way that helps your customer succeed. One of the biggest mistakes salespeople make is failing to take time to listen. This includes listening to prospects and listening to colleagues and competitors for advice. Embrace the fact that you do not know what you do not know. Salespeople who have the ability to truly listen and understand the customer and the industry will have the ability to be knowledgeable and problem solve in a meaningful way.

Unfortunately, what passes for listening today is waiting long enough for the speaker to finish before you have the chance to jump in and show them how smart you are. But the reality is, you need to do more than hear what they say. You need to understand what they mean.

Listening well requires brushing up on active listening skills:

1. Be present. That is, stay focused on your conversation and remove distractions.

2. Paraphrase often. Repeat what you hear back to your prospect.

3. Focus outside, not inside. Focus on what the prospect is

saying, not what you are going to say next.

4. Try thinking aloud. Voice your thoughts along the way out loud so you can determine whether you and your prospect are on the same page.

At a high level, respectful listening requires going beyond absorbing what you are hearing. It involves genuinely caring about the person you are speaking with. This means transcending information exchange to empathize with your prospect.

Respectful listening has three levels:

1. Get Data: Pay attention to the facts that your prospect shared.

2. Get Context: Take time to identify why that is meaningful.

3. Acknowledge: Take what you have learned and acknowledge its significance.

Three-level listening will help you build trust with your clients, remember more about them, and encourage them to share more with you.

SALES AS A SERVICE

"To win in today's world, every business has to transform themselves to become maniacally focused on the customer experience" Shantanu Narayen, CEO, Adobe

One of the more influential people in Mark's career is Charlie Green, the founder of Trusted Advisor Associates (TrustedAdvisor. com). Charlie has dedicated his career to writing, speaking, and consulting regarding the role trust plays in sales. Charlie believes that trust is the single most powerful factor driving client relationship effectiveness. Mark worked closely with Charlie at The Mac Group, a Harvard-based strategy consulting firm where

Charlie was a senior executive leading the merger and business transformation into Gemini Consulting and Mark was early into his career in sales and business development.

Charlie's thoughts on the importance of being a trusted advisor helped shape the way Mark has functioned as a salesperson right from the start. Charlie believes that if you change your goal from getting the sale to helping the client, the sale itself becomes a byproduct, not the goal. Paradoxically, if you focus on helping the client you get more sales.

Ultimately, the takeaway is this: sales is a win-win opportunity when you spend your time serving your customers and building trust rather than tricking your customers into buying. It's important to think of it this way: you are not selling something to someone, you are collaborating with your prospect to solve a problem.

This quote from Mark Roberge, former CRO, HubSpot and founder of Stage 2 Capital, depicts this thought process well:

"You know you are running a modern sales team when selling feels more like the relationship between a doctor and a patient and less like a relationship between a salesperson and a prospect. When you go in to see your doctor and she asks you about your symptoms, you tell her the truth. You trust that she can diagnose your problem and prescribe the right medication. When she says, 'This is what you have. Take these pills,' you don't say, 'Let me think about it' or 'Can I get 20 percent off?' You take the medication. It's no longer about interrupting, pitching, and closing. It is about listening, diagnosing, and prescribing."

One of the defining traits of being an empathetic salesperson who actively listens is to continually ask yourself how you can better serve the person you are interacting with (whether that's a colleague, a prospect, or a current customer). It requires asking yourself, what can I do to make this person's life easier? Or, asking them directly.

When you focus your energy on serving your prospects, they will naturally begin to think of you as a resource who is in their corner rather than someone who is pushing them to do something they do not want to do.

Leading in the sales world of tomorrow requires approaching sales as a service, not a one-time transaction. This approach requires knowing how your product or service can benefit your customer and always working to add value to your customer, breeding long-term client loyalty.

Good rules of thumb to keep in mind to be a better servant for your clients include:

- Have your client's best interest at heart.
- Seek to understand their interests.
- Offer advice that is useful to your client.
- Operate on their timeline, not yours.
- Be completely transparent and honest.
- Stay engaged post-sale to ensure your customer's success.
- Be proactive.
- Sell by doing, not telling.

When you do these things, your prospects will naturally feel more comfortable buying from you.

This means sales presentations and calls take a back seat to delivering actual value to your client. Your value will be apparent in your actions, not your words. For example, if you are working with a prospect with very complex needs, begin working with them for free (Selling by Doing, not Selling by Telling) or within a minor consulting engagement to build a relationship with them and illustrate the value of your product or service. In the software world, taking live data from a customer and working it into your demo or giving them free preliminary access to the tool is a great way to engage a prospect and add value.

SELL BY DOING WHENEVER YOU CAN

A few years ago, Mark was working with a prospect for over 6 months. This prospect would not sign a deal, despite his strongest efforts. Mark resigned himself to the notion that it was not going to happen. In fact, Mark planned to tell his CEO that he intended to pull the proposal. However, he couldn't shake the knowledge that he knew his solution would deliver a strong ROI for the prospect. Mark decided to try one more approach, one that would show the CRO that this purchase could positively impact the company and even change the trajectory of his career.

Mark offered the prospect four pro bono days of their product and consulting experts to work with the prospect's sales operation team to test the solution. The timing panned out, the CRO initially said no, but called back and said, "If you can start Monday, we'll give it a shot." Of course, the request happened the Wednesday before Thanksgiving. Regardless, Mark and his team worked like crazy over the holiday weekend to build a plan to sway the prospect.

Because Mark approached the sale with his client's needs in mind and did his best to try to go above and beyond to deliver the prospect value, he was awarded the deal on the third day of the four-day trial period. When the prospect saw the work in action, they couldn't deny the value. Therefore, sell by doing whenever you can.

REMEMBER THAT EVERY INTERACTION MATTERS.

Every new interaction is a chance to build a relationship and your own reputation. To build trust with prospects and gain respect, you must always, always, always engage sincerely. Maya Angelou's famous quote, "People will forget what you said, people will forget what you did, but people will never forget how you made them feel," is applicable here. The best way to make your prospects and customers feel good is to be consistently authentic, credible, reliable, and humble.

A few pointers to boost the impact of your interactions include:

1. Pick up the phone or, better yet, meet in person to have a conversation. Too much happens via text or email. We are all busy, but it goes a long way to make time to spend time with your prospects personally.

2. Keep your tone positive. If you are always positive with your connections, they will associate you with positivity.

3. Make eye contact. Eye contact is extremely important when establishing a personal connection.

Remember, your communication does not stop with verbal and text communication. Non-verbal communication matters too. Body language and your appearance both give your prospects clues about your authenticity and investment in what you are selling.

A great example of the importance of visual communication is the 1960 Nixon/Kennedy televised presidential debate. They were broadcast live on both TV and radio. Nixon was not feeling physically well the day of the debate and looked tired, pale, and had bouts of perspiration. But Nixon was a smart guy and held his own in the debate. In fact, people who listened to the debates on the radio judged Nixon to be the winner of the debates. However, people who watched the televised version said Kennedy—the younger, handsome, perspiration-free candidate—won the debate. The visual appearance mattered then, and it matters now.

Sports enthusiasts are aware of the fundamentals of non-verbal communication. We've all seen it and probably cheered. At your next baseball game, watch the catcher use every motion but mouth and lip coordination to indicate to the pitcher the optimal next play.

Hockey players fake a wrist shot when they aim to slam a slapshot in the left upper corner of the net.

During a football game, the quarterback receives the snap and takes three steps backwards, intending to throw a 25-foot pass to his favorite wide receiver. One step, two, and SLAM, he is forced to the ground, fans are cheering, and the announcer shouts, "A quarterback SACK!"

How did the defense break through the front line and take down the team captain? Simple, he watched for the non-verbal evidence; it could be the nod, the wrist motion, or the eyes. Or, as was the case with Nixon and Kennedy, it may be the sweat.

CHAPTER TAKEAWAYS

TAP INTO YOUR SOFT SIDE

Most buying decisions are emotional. People who are emotionally intelligent are likable, enthusiastic, and trustworthy. People buy from people they like. Thus, it is important to appeal to your prospects emotions, not just their logic.

TIPS FOR TAPPING INTO YOU SOFT SIDE:

- Listen more than you speak. Put yourself in your customer's shoes.

- Don't be afraid to be vulnerable. Take responsibility for mistakes and acknowledge shortcomings.

- Keep your own emotional state in mind. Make stress reduction and mindfulness a priority.

OWN THE FACT THAT YOUR PRIMARY RESPONSIBILITY IS LISTENING

One of the biggest mistakes salespeople make is failing to take time to listen. Salespeople who have the ability to truly listen and understand the customer and the industry will have the ability to be knowledgeable and problem solve in a meaningful way.

TIPS FOR BECOMING A BETTER LISTENER:

- Be present. Focus on the conversation at hand. Focus on what your prospect is saying, not what you are going to say next.

- Think aloud. Repeat what you are hearing back to your prospect. Voice your thoughts along the way so you can determine if you are on the same page.

- Use "Three-level" listening:

  1. Get Data: Pay attention to the facts that your prospect shared.

  2. Get Context: Take time to identify why that is meaningful.

  3. Acknowledge: Take what you have learned and acknowledge its significance.

Three-level listening will help you build trust with your clients, remember more about them, and encourage them to share more with you.

SERVE RATHER THAN SELL

When you focus your energy on serving your prospects rather than selling them, they will naturally begin to think of you as a resource who is in their corner rather than someone who is pushing them to do something they do not want to do.

TIPS FOR BEING A BETTER SERVANT FOR YOUR CLIENTS:

- Get involved in tough discussions. Don't shy away from challenging discussions. Instead, offer applicable solutions as soon as possible.

- Don't sell and run. Stay engaged and attentive to ensure your customer's success, even after they sign on the dotted line.

- Sell by doing, not by telling. The sooner you can start providing a service, the better. Always show your trustworthiness through your actions, not words alone.

CLOUD TITAN:
CATHY MINTER, CRO OF R3

The Power of Empathy to Drive Success as Well as Personal Well-Being

ABOUT CATHY MINTER

Cathy Minter has worked in software sales for 25 years. Cathy earned her Bachelor of Arts from Clemson University and went on to complete her Master of Business Administration at Fordham Gabelli School of Business. She began her career at AT&T, moving on to lead sales teams at Oracle, SAP, Cordys, SpaceTime Insight (acquired by Nokia), and Docker, Inc. before moving on to serve as CRO at R3, a DLT and blockchain software. Over the course of her career, working as a single mother and one of the only female leaders in a male-dominated industry, she learned the power of taking your time to learn along the path to sales success.

Cathy Minter spent the last 25 years working her way up the software sales leadership ladder. Balancing the demands of motherhood and corporate culture, Cathy chose a slower path than many of her male professional counterparts. She turned down promotions along the way and trusted that the opportunities would be there for her when she was ready so long as she kept working hard and learning each step of the way. She believes the slower path is not equivalent to complacency or not living up to your professional potential; it is pausing to stop, sharpen the scythe, and take every opportunity to learn along the way. And it was a crucial part of her sales success journey. She is successful—in part—because she has never been afraid to be humble or ask for help along the way.

Cathy gleaned this mindset from her Irish grandmother ("Nanny"), her greatest inspiration who represented the classic immigrant story: leaving her family in Ireland at age 17 and traveling to the U.S. by herself to start a better life. Nanny lived independently until the age of 95 and represented core values such as hard work, determination, persistence, flexibility, and, most of all, constant learning. Nanny was always looking to improve herself and her family with a humbleness and selflessness that inspired Cathy.

Cathy's mom relayed the story of her coming home from school one day to a sign on the door from Nanny, "I found a new and better place to live. We are now living around the corner please come over after school." That always brought some laughs around the dinner table hearing that old favorite tale, but the point was one that always rang true: always learn and improve. Cathy brought those values to the business world and they guide her both on an individual and leadership level. From her early days selling at Oracle, to now one of too few female chief revenue officers at an enterprise SaaS company, R3, Cathy credits her sales success to this philosophy.

Cathy was born and raised in the New Jersey suburbs of New York City. She was the youngest of three girls and a competitive athlete her whole life. The lessons she learned early in life have served her well throughout her professional life. One of her earliest accomplishments was making the 12-year-old little league all-star team, one of the only girls ever to do so at that time. From a young age, Cathy was comfortable performing outside of her comfort zone in situations way before they became commonplace.

She remembers the moms of the boys on her team always giving her an extra cheer and encouragement during the games and she didn't realize until later in life, coming out of the 70s decade of the feminist movement, just how happy they were to see a girl out there playing at the same level as their sons.

Ten years later, Cathy entered the business world during the first Gulf War; jobs right out of college were scarce. She was able to get in as an entry-level salesperson at AT&T post divestiture (when they were transforming the organization from a government monopoly to corporate enterprise). She learned quickly and moved up the ranks fast, gaining four promotions in five years, from commercial sales rep, to national account manager, to data network specialist, and finally Global Account Manager for Goldman Sachs, one of AT&T's largest customers.

The AT&T Branch Manager at the time had heard of something called the "World Wide Web." Cathy, the youngest person in the office and eager to help, was transferred to a small closet in NYC with a bunch of boxes around her, a large computer, six America Online floppy disks, and a bunch of cords. She spent three days trying, unsuccessfully, to connect internet service and had to deliver the news to her boss that she failed. This was in 1995. The Internet in the business world was just arriving.

During her time at AT&T, Cathy was attending graduate school at night in NYC when she ran into a friend who had gotten a job at Oracle. After researching the company and hearing about the huge potential for sales reps there, she tracked down the Regional Account Director at Oracle that ran the AT&T account. Cathy figured she could parlay her AT&T experience into selling Oracle to AT&T. After many months of closed doors, a position opened up and her career in enterprise software started. The pace and intensity of Oracle was a big leap from AT&T at the time. She soon experienced her first weekly forecast calls, which were affectionately referred to as "the woodchipper," and what became six years of intensely stressful quarter closes.

At the close of her first year at Oracle, she had so much anxiety and stress when her deal did not close on time that she walked out of the office, got sick to her stomach in the parking lot. But She picked herself up and stuck with it. She credits an amazing group of sales leaders that mentored and taught her that adversity brings the greatest growth and learning. It was then that she leaned into the fact that empathy for yourself, your colleagues, and for your customers is really what drives success in sales.

Over those six years at Oracle, she had two children, sold close to $100M in software, and was later recruited over to SAP's communication industry sales team. Eighteen months later she was promoted to Sales VP for the communication industry in the US. The further up in leadership she climbed, the more of a minority she was as a female. She also struggled balancing being a single mom and executive, trying to do everything for everyone and not necessarily feeling like she was doing any of it to 100%. Her saving grace was having empathy for herself and focusing on what she loved most about her work to motivate her: her passion for emerging tech, working for great people, and the start-up mentality. She found that by focusing on delivering bottom line results (versus the politics of a larger corporation) she was more satisfied at work, she learned more, and she became more successful too.

After five years at SAP, Cathy made a risky move in 2008 when the cloud was nascent. In fact, most company executives promised never to move secure data "into an unsecure cloud" environment. Cathy's bet on herself paid off. She spent the next ten years at two emerging tech start-ups. One was Cordys, a cloud-based business process management company where she was President of the Americas. The other was SpaceTime, a data analytics, IOT (later AI-focused) platform company. Cathy's prior boss at SAP, Rob Schilling, worked with SpaceTime and called her to "get the gang back together." After going through three CEOs and a financial crash in 2008, Cathy recognized the power of a mantra she now always follows: work for the person, not the company. Working for someone you respect and learn from is key to job happiness and success.

At Spacetime, as employee number 25 at a brand-new start up, she remembers going back to her roots as an individual contributor and at that time that greatly simplified her work/life balance. They needed to land new business and they got an introduction to FedEx. As she described it, she grabbed her founder (her SE), her CMO (her product guy), and herself (AE) and made trips to Memphis to close a deal worth over $4M; at the time, the company had under $500K in sales a year. This put them on the map and she soon built up a sales and Professional Services team of close to 80 people globally. The highlight was a 3 am tour of the FedEx hub in Memphis, watching the hundreds of planes land and take off, an incredible operation, knowing the software they provided was now powering FedEx's new global planning systems.

Years later, as head of Americas Sales for Docker, Cathy moderated a session for Women in Tech. The highlighted speaker was Francine Gordon, PhD, a veteran silicon valley figure and professor at Santa Clara University. She described what Cathy looked back on as "imposter syndrome," and soon realized that many people experience what she had throughout her career. It was a turning point for Cathy to realize that she was not alone in her struggles to balance work and life; that if you focus primarily on working hard, never settling but not rushing, and learning along the way, you will succeed.

This approach paid off for Cathy over her twenty-year path to a c-suite position at an enterprise software company. When a prior board member from SpaceTime recommended her for a job at a growing "blockchain" company, recognizing that it was headed into some of the most emerging tech out there, it ended up being the perfect opportunity for Cathy. It brought her back to NYC where she grew up and it requires that she leverage every single skill set she ever learned, from the utility closet at AT&T to being MC at a large tech event for Docker. With her kids in college now, Cathy believes the best is yet to come in her career as a software sales leader.

CATHY'S TIPS:

IT'S EASIER TO SELL ASPIRIN THAN VITAMINS

In sales, you should always be solving a business problem. Know your prospect's pain points and offer a solution that helps solve them. Your prospects want tangible solutions to the problems they face every day, not a promise of a potential solution that you think they need.

IT'S NOT ABOUT YOUR QUOTA, IT'S ABOUT HOW YOU TREAT PEOPLE

Customer relationships will make or break your career. You should always focus on how you treat people and do what is best for your relationship, not for your sales quota. I've had more success and call-backs from being thoughtful and empathetic than from attempting to make hard sales.

ENTERPRISE DEALS DIE MANY DEATHS BEFORE THEY GET DONE

The larger the deal, the more complicated the sales cycle. Every time a deal dies, celebrate... you are getting closer! The right fits will work out in the end with consistent and determined effort.

BE THE GLUE

Help your customers align disparate groups; don't assume (or wait) for them to do it themselves.

DON'T EVER COMPROMISE YOUR INTEGRITY

No matter what you do, ensure it lines up with your core values. Be honest. Work hard. Have heart. Trust the process.

#4 AUTHENTICITY

ARE YOU THE REAL DEAL, OR ARE YOU A GOOD ACT? YOUR PROSPECTS NOTICE.

"Be yourself—not your idea of what you think somebody else's idea of yourself should be."

- Henry David Thoreau

As sales professionals, we are always on the lookout for opportunities to connect with our customers, clients, and channel partners. There are countless sales manuals filled with tips and tricks to make connections. However, we believe there is one common-sense approach that works wonders: be yourself. It may seem too simple, but we promise it's effective. Best of all, it's easy to stick to because it comes naturally. When you focus on staying true to your values and your personality in your sales message, you'll naturally be on your way to building trust with your customers. That is because customers can sense when you are being genuine.

When you ditch any effort to act a certain prescribed way, you are free to follow your gut. Your gut will often lead you to your customer's actual pain points. When you are genuine and understand your customer's pain points, you come across as a trusted advisor, not a salesperson chasing a commission.

Additionally, authenticity is increasingly important as more companies prioritize culture. Your prospects want to buy from companies that align with their values. Many companies place integrity, honesty, and trust at the top of their value list. When you serve a company that aligns with your values, your job gets a lot easier and a lot more fulfilling.

We live in a world where short-term interactions (like texts and social media) are commonplace. However, playing the long game is more important than ever. Investing time and energy in one-on-one meetings, phone calls, and travel is worthwhile because it drives genuine human connection, and genuine human connection drives sales.

Authenticity means doing everything with pure intentions, being unafraid to be vulnerable and take risks, and being open. This approach will not only help you win deals, it will also give you peace of mind and fulfillment.

BE TRUE TO YOURSELF

Have you ever felt you were spinning a tall-tale as a salesperson? If so, how did that go for you? Likely, if it delivered any success at all, it was short term. Authenticity is a longer game than spin, but it delivers tenfold. Authenticity breeds referrals and positive word-of-mouth, both inside and outside of your organization. Positive word of mouth is important because, while good news travels fast, bad news travels faster.

We've all seen examples of people trying to act sincere. More often than not, it is clear when someone doesn't have pure intentions. Success in business isn't "seeing how much you can get away with." Authentically successful people are true to themselves and have pure intentions when communicating with others.

Consider this: Do you know someone who...

- Is wonderful to listen to?
- Is relaxed and real?

- Seems glad to hear what you have to say?

- Always tells the truth?

- Keeps their promises?

If you do, you know an authentically successful person. Regardless of title or salary, if you embody these qualities, you embody success.

When we reflect on our most successful colleagues, they have always been the people who value character, loyalty, respect, and authenticity. More than that, they are people who are quick on their feet and dedicated to gradually building knowledge about our trade.

While some "sales reps" are less than honest and in the business for a quick buck, most of us chose sales because we enjoy the challenge, need the variety, and thrive on the pace of this work. The leaders in our profession enjoy building lasting relationships with the people they serve. It might sound grandiose, but the philosophy is simple: be yourself and act with pure intentions and you will be successful in sales.

Jim Jensen, SVP Global Partners and Alliances at Ceridian and former CIO of Ultimate Software says "most sales representatives make this much harder than it needs to be. They believe that to be successful in sales, they have to reinvent themselves into something else. That doesn't work. To be successful in life and business you need to always be you".

Jim has learned over a successful career that he is really an introvert by nature that does well and even is energized by his more extrovert-driven parts of his business day. However, he needs to structure his workday to include alone time where he designs corporate strategy, analyzes the performance of his team and builds his approach for his next executive sales call or corporate presentation. Any other way for Jim would blunt the impact he brings to the companies

KNOW YOUR OWN STORY

Perspective and mindset are critical in sales. A surefire way to have an authentic mindset and genuine perspective is to know where you come from, where you're going, and the "why" behind everything you do. Simon Sinek popularized the concept of knowing your "Why" in his book Start with Why in 2009. However, the heart of the concept is connected to an age-old question: what is our purpose in life? It's a question both companies and individuals should ask themselves.

Knowing your Why means understanding what you stand for and what matters most to you. Beyond that, it means living in alignment with that understanding. Owning your Why is crucial in sales because humans buy from humans and our fellow humans care about our motivations. As Sinek explains, "People don't buy what you do, they buy why you do it." Therefore, when we are aware of our Why, we are better able to connect with and sell to others.

When you are in touch with your true north, you are more likely to find an employer that aligns with your values. If your values do not line up with the values of the company or product you are selling, it is unlikely you will find any sustainable success. Despite that fact, many of us compromise our "why" for money, connections, or acceptance. How often have you found yourself at odds with the vision you verbalize to your team or family? The stories we tell and the visions we share are not always our truth.

To illustrate that point, consider how many would-be musicians become lawyers to please their parents or the mechanics who work in their parent's business while they dream of a different life.

Today, there are still many cultures where individuals are promised to suitors who please the ambitions a parent may have for their child, leaving that young man or woman without a love story of their own. The same misalignments happen in sales. Tuning into your truth and ensuring your company's Why is in alignment with yours will be critical to your long-term success.

When is the last time you assessed whether your career and life align with your authentic self? If you do not take time to assess this and make changes, you can end up resenting aspects of your life. When you carry resentment, you may sabotage your own efforts with sickness and relational or emotional difficulty.

To that end, remember that you will spend half your life working. Knowing that, isn't it worthwhile to work with and for people you enjoy? Toxic culture begets toxicity. Your gut will tell you when you are in a bad situation where people or the company doesn't align with your values.

When you follow your gut, you will find your way to a rewarding career environment. Know your Why, tell yourself the truth, and meld your motive and the methodology to manifest your own success. Once you understand your personal mission, you can integrate your dreams and others' expectations into a story that is mutually beneficial.

Furthermore, do not be afraid to be vulnerable and share your story. Take risks with relationships and be completely open. This is important because there is no trust without risk. Someone has to take the first risk. If you only focus on being trustworthy, you depend on the other party to take a risk. That is the sales equivalent of "aggressively waiting for the phone to ring." You simply can't count on your prospect being vulnerable with you if you are not vulnerable and open to taking risks yourself.

KNOW THEIR STORY

As we discussed in the chapter on empathy, your story is not the only story you should be tuned in to, especially with enterprise-level sales. You do not sell a commodity. The buying decisions made around enterprise-level software sales are career defining for our buyers. Often a prospect's career advancement or failure is on the line when a project is implemented. Our buyers are not looking for a plug-and-play solution. They are looking for a technology partner who will implement the solution well and support them beyond implementation.

To be successful in connecting with our buyers, we need to get the full story affecting their decision. Make sure you understand:

- How will buying our technology improve our buyer's career?
- What risk is my buyer taking by purchasing from us?
- What is motivating my buyer to look for a solution like ours?
- What level of involvement will the C-level at my prospect's company have in the decision?
- What are the primary factors driving this purchase process?
- How can I build trust with everyone involved in the process?
- What business outcomes do they hope to achieve with my solution?

The bigger the ticket, the less price matters. Our prospects are not buying based on price, they are buying based on gut feelings and perceived value. So, how can you differentiate? You can differentiate and build trust by aligning with your prospect's culture. When an executive is buying a transformational technology, they want to know the values of the company they are buying from. It is crucial that both the sales and delivery team understand the customer's needs and build intimacy and trust with the ultimate buyer. This means taking the time to listen to what's really important to the individual and aligning with their actual needs. The reality is most technologies are similar. The differentiator that remains is how you treat people and how you make them feel. This is why culture is a topic increasingly popping up in RFPs.

LEARN TO WALK AWAY

"Saying yes to everything will kill you slowly and softly."
- Stephanie Melish

If your culture doesn't align with a prospect's, learn to walk away. Let's be clear: there is nothing wrong with understanding a client's needs, matching your service or product to those needs, and working through objections and concerns while doing so. However, many of us believe we have the ability to coerce a prospect into buying based on sales skills and determination. This is where we fall off the track.

When we work too hard to change decisions, we lose sight of the bigger picture. A major key to your sales success is your network and industry reputation. Don't forget that coercion and over-aggressiveness erode your network and industry reputation over time.

Don't push too hard. Instead, learn to walk away professionally and unequivocally. Additionally, don't be afraid to recommend another firm that may be a better fit, even if they are a competitor. It will boost your reputation.

KEEP IN TOUCH AFTER "NO"

It turns out "no" is not such a terrible word. It teaches us a great deal. "No" can help train us to become the type of salesperson we want to be: a salesperson with integrity, honesty, and truly productive relationships with his or her clients. The key is to learn from every "no," and to keep in touch with prospects after "no."

Keeping in touch after "no" is not foolish goodwill. Instead, it is a solution that will take you away from an us-versus-them mentality to a new mindset that allows you to consistently build relationships and account momentum with your clients.

"No" doesn't have to be the end of the road. For example, Paul once lost out on a deal after a sophisticated RFP to a large player in the software industry. Paul's company had a salesperson involved in the deal that the prospect hadn't jived with. The competitor who won the deal had made a lot of big promises, and Paul had an inkling that they may not be able to deliver on those promises. Instead of shutting the door completely or making excuses, he gracefully bowed out and thanked the prospect for the opportunity. He took a humble approach and apologized for his colleague's behavior. He asked if it would be OK if he checked in once a month on the project status. Fast forward nine-months, the client wasn't happy with the work being done. Paul set up a meeting with them and ended up winning a $20 million deal. In the end, putting his ego aside, being humble, and being patient helped him close the deal.

Bottom line: do not burn bridges. The sales world is smaller than you think. You never know what team you will be playing on in the future. People move around a lot. If you stay in software sales for decades, it is not unusual to sell to the same person three or four times in your career at three or four different companies.

CHAPTER TAKEAWAYS

BE TRUE TO YOURSELF

Authenticity means doing everything with pure intentions, staying open minded to your prospect's perspective, being honest with yourself and others, and knowing when to walk away. This approach will not only help you win deals, it will give peace of mind and fulfillment.

TIPS FOR BEING A MORE AUTHENTIC SALESPERSON:

- Always be honest. Truth breeds referrals and positive word of mouth. Spin doesn't. Also, it's just a lot easier than remembering which lie you told to which individual.

- Always have pure intentions. When your intentions are pure, you will be relaxed and real and your customers will take note.

KNOW YOUR "WHY"

A surefire way to have an authentic mindset and genuine perspective is to know where you come from, where you are going, and the "why" behind everything you do. Knowing your why means understanding what you stand for and what matters most to you, and living in alignment with that understanding.

TIPS FOR UNCOVERING AND EMBRACING YOUR "WHY"

Ask yourself:

- What motivates you?

- What about your work brings you joy?

- What is your personal mission?

- Do the answers to the first three questions align with what you do at work each day?

DON'T BE AFRAID TO WALK AWAY

Many of us believe we have the ability to coerce a prospect into buying based on sales skills and determination. This is where we get off track. We maximize our capacity for success when we walk away from deals that aren't good fits.

TIPS FOR KNOWING WHEN TO WALK AWAY:

- Focus on quality over quantity. A full pipeline is worthless if it is full of low-quality opportunities. Pursuing a lead is time consuming. Always analyze a lead before investing a firm's resources to chase it.

- Be honest about your company's strength and shortfalls. It's better to be honest and up-front and recommend another firm than to under deliver.

A TRIBUTE TO BILL CAMPBELL - THE TRILLION DOLLAR COACH

From a beleaguered college football coach (12-41-1) at Boston College and Columbia University to an executive coach that helped create over $2 trillion of enterprise business value.

ABOUT BILL

Bill was a software and technology sales and marketing leader at leading tech companies, including Apple, Claris, Intuit, and GO Corporation. Over the course of his career, he coached some of the most revered executives at tech giants such as Google, Amazon, eBay, Yahoo, Twitter, and Facebook, including Larry Page, Steve Jobs, Jeff Bezos, Marissa Mayer, Dick Costolo, and Sheryl Sandberg, among others.

Bill Campbell embodied authenticity. He was not only Mensa-level brilliant, clairvoyant, and an incredibly gifted athlete, but also, and most importantly, he was a truly authentic person who found ways to communicate with, influence, and impact others in ways others have not.

Mark was introduced to Bill by a private equity partner who was a mutual friend. He quickly learned first-hand how special he was. Mark asked him for help with some research he was doing for a project he was working in concert with Duke (University) Corporate Education. Mark fully expected he might say he was too busy, just not able to help, or just slow down his responsiveness to him in a way that conveyed that he wasn't so excited to add work to a very busy schedule.

However, that wasn't Bill. He said yes. Now that Mark had the pleasure of knowing him, albeit for too short a period of time (Bill lost a battle with cancer in 2016), he can't imagine him saying no.

Although Mark and Bill didn't have the time to get to know each other extremely well, he always responded to Mark's emails and calls, and would occasionally just reach out to check-in. He would always ask about his family, business, and was always game to discuss if the Columbia Lions football team (that he once coached, and Mark was recruited to play for) would ever have a winning record again. Sadly, they did in 2017, one year after his passing. We wonder if Bill had anything to do with that.

Bill was as authentic as they get. Even in front of his sometimes aloof and always proper business colleagues, he would tone down his use of profanity, not one bit. He never put on a facade. He once asked Mark if he ever cursed around old friends or family members and Mark answered that for some reason, he just has never cursed much in his life. He seemed to appreciate that Mark was the same person pretty much no matter the setting, but Mark could tell he thought it was a little odd. Cursing was part of his authentic personality and he wasn't going to change that for anyone. That's about the best description of authenticity that we have ever experienced.

We unequivocally recommend the book about Bill's incredible life achievements, "Trillion Dollar Coach". In the book, authors Eric Schmidt, Jonathan Rosenberg, and Alan Eagle do a wonderful job sharing how Bill so positively impacted Silicon Valley and how he can help you and us become more successful, authentic selling professionals as well.

TOP TIPS FOR AUTHENTICITY—BILL CAMPBELL

- Don't assume your employees automatically respect you because you're the boss.
- Do what's right, even if it's unpopular.
- It's not about you, it's about the team.
- Care about courage and getting things done more than egos and IQs.
- The aggregate is more powerful than anything you can come up with alone.
- Ask for the best ideas, not consensus.
- Park your ego. Life and business are team sports.
- A great player makes the team stronger, not the stand-out player.
- Leaders are completely there in everything they do.
- Treat everyone with dignity, even in failure.
- Always be available.

CLOUD TITAN
JOE FUCA, CEO AT
REPUTATION.COM

Using Authenticity and Grit to Coach a Culture of Success Throughout a Company

ABOUT JOE

Joe is a 30-year hardened veteran of the technology and SaaS industry. He served as the world-wide sales leader for DocuSign, President of Financial Force, and is currently CEO at Reputation. com. Over the course of his career, Joe has led some of the most successful SaaS businesses through major growth phases and directed enterprise-level sales, implementation, and customer success groups. He is known for his ability to innovate SaaS processes to ensure client satisfaction. At DocuSign, Joe helped establish the company's brand globally, grew recurring revenue ten-fold, and developed strategic partnerships with Salesforce and some of the world's most successful consulting firms.

THE IMPORTANCE OF AUTHENTIC LEADERSHIP

Joe Fuca knows a thing or two about authenticity and grit. After serving as a four-year football starter and earning two degrees (in Business and Communication Arts) at California Lutheran University, Joe raised four children with his wife of 31 years and led several leading enterprise software companies through major transition phases, always delivering outstanding growth.

Over the course of his career, Joe has built world-class teams and built relationships with renowned investors. Like Liam Neeson's character in the Taken movies, Joe has amassed a very particular set of skills that are a nightmare to his competitors. He has mastered the art of inspiring others through trust, honesty, strength of character, and authentic leadership. He credits his coach-like mindset for his success.

So, what does it mean to have a coach-like mindset? To Joe, just like Bill, it means advocating for a winning culture and having a team of pinch-hitting team members with the grit to succeed. That means a work culture that is focused on cultivating positive attitudes, holding team members to high standards, and aligning team members to give their all to achieve shared goals. Winning teams are honest with each other, authentic, and well-equipped to handle adversity. Winning teams are always well-coached and trained; always authentic and real; and always built around individuals with strong ethics, high character, intelligence, and grit.

Another aspect of Joe's leadership style is his prioritization of authenticity. One story he shared that illustrated the importance of authenticity came from his time at Docusign. In 2014, T-Mobile was growing quickly and their CMO Mike Sievert (now CEO of T-Mobile)reached out to DocuSign. He was worried that they had no way to process orders fast enough inside the store and no mechanism for documenting them in an electronic format. T-Mobile was very forward-thinking at the time and were running many promotions that were disrupting the behemoths in the industry at the time: AT&T and Verizon. They were dealing with an extremely high number of point-of-sale transactions. The deal they were discussing with Docusign was game changing at the time. Docusign had not done an 8-figure deal for an annual contract and this deal would have far exceeded that. Since it was new territory, Joe and his team had to be honest and authentic about the risk involved with this type of scale and complexity. They brought in their CTO to make adjustments to the platform to handle the volume and speed T-Mobile needed. They needed to have orders processed and contracts recorded on an iPad in less than 2 minutes in the stores. Joe and his team suggested a pilot and ran into many challenges along the way, all of which they communicated about honestly. T-Mobile appreciated their honest approach and they signed Docusign's largest contract in history. Joe attributes this massive sale to the authenticity of more than 20 people on his team throughout their entire 1-year sales cycle with T-Mobile and for many years after that.

If you are looking to build an authentic team that can close deals like this one, Joe suggests putting potential hires through the "meal test." The test is simple: share a meal with them and evaluate whether their heart and attitude is focused on playing the long game, or playing the short game. Authentic coaches want long-game players.

JOE'S TIPS

- Feverishly build strategic relationships with partners, advisors, and industry experts. This means investing heavily in verticals and your overall ecosystem.

- Hire employees that can handle adversity (those with GRIT). Traits to look for include those who value trust, honest, and character.

- Be a coach, not just a manager. This means having the courage to take risks, be curious, and always be authentically you. Your team will respect it.

CREATIVITY & PROBLEM SOLVING

#5

THE IMPORTANCE OF THINKING OUTSIDE THE BOX AND STORYTELLING

"Making the simple complicated is commonplace; making the complicated simple, awesomely simple, that's creativity."

- Charles Mingus

Sales professionals are not necessarily grouped with "creative types," but sales greats are certainly creative innovators. Strict quotas and cold-call plans may not leave much room for out-of-the-box thinking, but as problem solving and storytelling gain ground as effective (and expected) sales skills, the importance of ingenuity in sales is growing too.

The days of one-size-fits-all approaches to selling are over. Today—especially in the world of enterprise-level software sales—every sale should be approached with creative and consultative lenses. Our customers do not expect a kit-solution. They are looking for a technology that is well suited to their individual needs, their current systems, and their future goals.

In response to these trends, we need to bid farewell to boilerplate sales pitches and pre-packaged demos. Instead, we need to embrace storytelling to connect and actively listen to glean the knowledge we need to be true problem solvers for our clients.

Customers are not looking for another salesperson to list the features and benefits of a product or service. They are looking for a creative problem solver who can understand their desired business outcomes and help them achieve them. Success as a creative salesperson means being an effective problem solver, a moving storyteller, and a motivating coach.

BE A PROBLEM SOLVER

In the ever-evolving world of enterprise software sales, it is our duty to adapt with the latest technology and continually customize our offerings to meet our customer's unique needs and objections. A whole new world of sales success will become available to you when you stop focusing on making sales and instead on solving problems.

Solving problems requires creating value and connection by understanding what your prospect needs and going out of your way to customize a solution for them. Don't be stymied by a set-in-stone process. Instead, be open to working alongside your customer. Today's buyers are advanced. They know more about your product and your competitors' products than ever before. We are no longer the educator armed with information; we are problem solvers armed with good questions. Our job is to listen closely to our customers and cater our solutions to their needs. And our jobs don't end at implementation. Today, we are expected to engage and ensure long-term customer success, forming long-term partnerships, evolving with and for our clients and partners.

If a customer or partner sees a limitation in your solution, creative salespeople are empowered to enhance their solution in such a way to address that limitation. To that end, as a salesperson, you stand at an especially important juncture for your company's success— you are a liaison between the market and your company. You have the power to make meaningful suggestions to improve your product to better serve the market.

When your customers point out any shortcomings of your solution, you have the opportunity to suggest that a new feature or integration be built to meet the customer's unique needs. Creative sales professionals are not limited by what is, they are open-minded to imagine what could be. They have connections to engineering leaders, internal product designers, and executives who can help shape the solution you offer to meet your customer's evolving needs. Remember, there is always another way and another opportunity to improve.

CONNECT THROUGH STORIES

When was the last time you were moved by a story? It was probably more recently than you realize. Stories are woven into the fabric of our personal and professional lives; they are in the music we play, the TED talks we watch, the articles we read, and the ads we hear.

It's well documented that human beings are moved by stories. We crave storylines and characters to which we can relate. Storytelling is important in sales because it humanizes your message. It is yet another way to genuinely connect with your prospects. It transforms your pitch into a conversation, and it helps you establish credibility with your prospect.

Modern neurological research finds that storytelling triggers the release of Oxytocin (often called the "trust hormone"). Oxytocin plays a significant role in social bonding. It is the neurochemical that promotes connection and encourages people to feel empathy. Not only that, but research shows that storytelling exceeds the power of pure data alone. One study found that storytelling activates seven regions of the brain, while data alone only activated two.[4] Knowing that, dare to move beyond bullet points to the great frontier of multi-dimensional, engaging stories.

We're not all naturally engaging storytellers. Fortunately, there are some basic tenets you can channel to improve your storytelling ability. Good stories have a clear introduction, middle, and conclusion. The best stories have a main character that faces a challenge and overcomes it.

A few common ways to leverage storytelling in sales include:

PERSONAL ANECDOTES

It's always helpful to establish common ground with your prospects. Sharing a personal story about your life or day that is relatable is a good way to build trust.

OVERCOMING OBJECTIONS

Address a prospect's objection by relaying a story about a former customer who felt a similar way and overcame it through purchasing your solution.

SHARING SUCCESS STORIES

Customer success stories are prime for story mining. A Gartner study found that 70% of executive buyers believe customer stories are the best way to differentiate a company from its competitors. Pro tip: bring up a customer the prospect knows, respects, or fears.

Overall, stories come more naturally with practice. You just need to start storytelling. Soon, you will learn which stories are the most moving.

Stories have helped us enormously in our career because they have allowed us to better understand our customers. In fact, we've

---

4. Snow, Joe Lazauskas and Shane. "The Strange Thing That Happens In Your Brain When You Hear a Good Story -- And How to Use It to Your Advantage." HubSpot Blog, 2018, blog. hubspot.com/marketing/the-strange-thing-that-happens-in-you-brain-when-you-hear-a-good-story-and-how-to-use-it-to-your-advantage.

found that tuning into the stories our customers tell us is even more important than telling stories of our own.

HERE'S AN EXAMPLE STORY TO ILLUSTRATE THE POINT:

I could feel the trickle of sweat beading and slowly inching its way down his chest. The sun was magnified through George's corner window; it was midday in July. I could have survived the sauna with more dignity had we not been trapped in that office for the past 42 minutes while Mr. George Paleirti, a new client, droned on about taxes, truck repairs, his brother's wife's phobias and his doubts about the future of the whole "global warming fiasco."

Clearly, we were making no progress with our proposed upgrades to his company's system and Clarence, his techie colleague, was ready to bolt. July in Phoenix is an oven on the best days, and today, we were cooked.

On the surface, I had to agree with Clarence's private eye rolls and eyebrow departure suggestions. George certainly appeared disinterested and almost paralyzed by the company's lackluster performance in the last two quarterly reports. You know that feeling when you know something, but you don't seem to know what it is? I had that feeling.

Adjusting my legs to angle myself in the draft of the nearest air conditioning vent, I saw the photo wall. I was not sure why it was new to me. I had been in George's office four or five times at that point and usually spent an hour or more in his company, but I had never seen this collection of photos.

There were snapshots of awards nights, children's birthday parties, George standing next to new machinery in the factory, George standing with two older gentlemen in what appeared to be a more "historic" rendition of his corner office, groundbreaking ceremonies, and even a photo of the older gentleman with a former senator of Arizona.

I had never inquired about the history of the company. "George," I asked, "Is this your family's business? Who are those two older guys with you in that photo?"

"Oh yeah," he replied with a quick hankie swipe across his forehead, "that's my pop and my granddad. Granddad built this business from nothing. In his day, he was a success story in Arizona. Look, you can see him with the senator in this photo. His innovative approach to mass bottle production won him the approval of his men and the ranking officials. He turned it over to my dad in 1956, and he brought modern teamwork to the floor. Together they built a winner!" You wouldn't know it looking at George's wearied face, his bloodshot eyes, and the veins visible in his cheeks.

Suddenly I knew what I knew. George's earlier monologue of complaints was a story of his fear. He was deeply concerned that, in the modern economy, he was not the innovator his granddad was and not the marketing man his dad became. George was a manager with a sagging factory, worn out from years of effort and persistence. It wasn't that he didn't want our software; George didn't want to lose the heritage his family had entrusted him with, and he lacked the bigger perspective to see possibilities for the future.

George's stories told me all I needed to know. I took off my software sales hat and became a business consultant that blistering day in July. That was four years ago. Today, George and his factory are renewed, not because of what I had to sell, but the stories we told each other.

LEARNING TO BE A STORYTELLER

It's important to learn from life's ups and downs. Paul and I have been favored with many incredible opportunities in this life in business as well as personally.

One very enjoyable and enlightening area, far-off from the enterprise software sales ecosystem, has been my exposure to the TV and film production industry, which started for me with a few long-time friends that became successful TV and film actors, and has evolved into a few very close relationships with a few successful producers and directors.

Through these relationships and some involvement in their productions, I learned an invaluable lesson. The most powerful and productive processes in business, as well as life in general, involve storytelling. Charts, graphs, and whiteboards are all great ways to communicate visually, but there is nothing that conveys the full descriptive emotion and details as effectively as a story.

Two of the absolute best storytellers I have ever met are Craig Singer and Flody Suarez.

Craig is an acclaimed film director and producer with a few indie blockbusters, like Animal Room, A Good Night to Die, and Dark Ride. Craig also sold his fan-driven Web/Interactive TV business to Disney and stayed on to run Disney Interactive and serve as creative director for over ten years.

Flody is a renowned TV and Broadway producer and show creator with successes like TV's The Eight Simple Rules for Dating My Teenage Daughter and Rise, as well as Broadway's The Cher Show.

You have not heard a story told if you have never listened to an accomplished director or producer like Craig or Flody pitch a show or movie. Maybe it is the creative talents that drew them into this business in the first place or how closely they connect to their creative concept, but it is uncanny how well the message comes across and how impactful it becomes.

You can be as powerful as a producer in a pitch meeting by accomplishing a few key things:

- Know your company story fully and why it is different/better than the competition.

- Know the WHY for your business, not just the HOW.

- Choose the company you work for wisely. You cannot have passion for a company, product, or a company's WHY unless you unequivocally connect to them.

- Learn how your products and services truly make your clients successful and also where it comes in short. Choose the company you work for wisely. Be transparent, authentic, emotional, honest, vulnerable, and passionate. Then tell your story.

Since everyone doesn't get to sit in a show or movie pitch, search around YouTube for real pitches (as compared to the comedic versions) that are out there. You'll see the energy, passion, and creativity first-hand.

Storytelling is a business, selling, and life superpower. Invest the time to learn to do it to the best of your ability.

CHAPTER TAKEAWAYS

BE A PROBLEM SOLVER

Customers are not looking for another salesperson to list features and benefits of a product or service. They are looking for a creative problem solver who can understand their desired business outcomes and help them achieve them.

TIPS FOR BEING A BETTER PROBLEM SOLVER:

- Don't focus on making sales. Focus on solving your prospects problems first. The sale will happen naturally.

- Take time to understand your prospects needs. Don't bring your standard solution to the table and tell the prospect what they need. Customize your offering and message to their needs.

CONNECT THROUGH STORIES

Human beings are moved by stories. We crave storylines and characters to which we can relate. Storytelling is important in sales because it humanizes your message. It is yet another way to genuinely connect with your prospects.

TIPS FOR LEVERAGING STORIES IN SALES:

- Use personal anecdotes. Sharing a personal story about your life or day that is relatable is a good way to build trust.

- Address objections by bringing up a story about a customer who felt similarly. Address a prospect's objection by relaying a story about a former customer who felt a similar way and overcame it through purchasing your solution.

- Share customer success stories. A Gartner study found that 70% of executive buyers believe customer stories are the best way to differentiate a company from its competitors.

CLOUD TITAN:
EILEEN M. VOYNICK, SOFTWARE SALES
EXECUTIVE, INDEPENDENT BOARD
DIRECTOR AT R3

Creativity Means Problem Solving

ABOUT EILEEN

Eileen Voynick has served in executive leadership roles at enterprise software companies for more than 25 years. Eileen has been a Chief Operating Officer, Chief Executive Officer, and board member for giants such as SAP, Oracle, Allscripts, Sparta Systems, and AdvancedMD. Eileen is a highly successful enterprise software industry executive, known for her ability to implement change leading to profitable growth and increased company valuation.

As CEO of Sparta Systems, a leading provider of enterprise quality management software solutions, she provided focused vision, leadership and strategic direction. As the Chief Operating Officer of Allscripts, a provider of clinical software, information and connectivity solutions for physicians, Eileen drove significant growth in profits and revenue and developed an extensive product portfolio. She was also instrumental in helping the company to successfully merge with Eclipsys, a $1.3 billion transaction.

In addition, Eileen was an Executive Vice President at SAP during its formative hyper growth years in the mid-1990's, improving revenue from $100 million to more than a $1 billion. In the mid-2000's, as Siebel Systems' Senior Vice President of Global Services, she had general manager responsibility and helped to create the Customer Experience Blueprint Program, which was later issued a U.S. patent. She subsequently joined Oracle's North American executive team as the SVP of Americas Consulting, a more than $1 billion organization with over 5,000 employees.

Today, Eileen is a member of the Board of Directors of CDK Global (Hoffman Estates, IL) and r3 (London). In addition, Eileen continues to mentor young women with a passion for their growth and development as future global leaders and entrepreneurs.

Eileen Voynick believes that being creative does not equate to artistic genius or outlandish ideas; instead, creativity is the embodiment of innovative problem solving. Thomas Edison once said, "Anything that won't sell, I don't want to invent. Its sale is proof of utility, and utility is success." To Voynick, creative thinking in sales and leadership works when it connects inventive ideas with something that is valuable and useful. True value and utility are the difference between a mere "invention" and a game-changing "INNOVATION." Essentially, connecting inventiveness with a business need is creativity.

Many salespeople aspire to move beyond the ranks of salesperson to a role as CRO and later to roles as CEO, COO, or Chairperson. As it turns out, the tenants that make you successful as a salesperson are also the characteristics that make you successful as a business leader, and one of those traits is, undoubtedly, creativity.

Sometimes being creative does not mean coming up with something completely new but improving products/systems that are already in use. In fact, one of Voynick's most powerful innovations was the repurpose of something that was already in place rather than a reinvent of the wheel. She led the launch of the Accelerated SAP methodology (ASAP Methodology) by restructuring tried-and-true SAP implementation approaches into a time-proven model that SAP and system integrators throughout the world use every day.

Similarly, in May 2010, her inventive work in streamlining customer experience at Siebel Systems led her to earn a U.S. patent for the Customer Experience Blueprint program. The methods and systems she and her team developed have helped Siebel Systems (and its acquirer Oracle Corporation) build one of the industry's greatest customer experiences with the highest customer satisfaction scores.

In fact, she was effectively carrying out a customer success strategy before it was called "customer success." She combined creativity with problem solving to better serve Siebel's customers by documenting what was working and configuring it into an innovative blueprint for the future. We consider Voynick one of the most impactful and successful creators of this key business function.

For example, Voynick believes that the reason Sparta had such a strong valuation both times they sold during her tenure as CEO was due to the customer success strategy. She and her team were able to illustrate their success by showing nearly a decade of their strategy patterns and demonstrating that it was a third easier to meet revenue goals by focusing on opportunities within their current customer base rather than pursuing new qualified leads. In fact, she found that she needed nearly three times the quota coverage on existing verticals and five times the quota coverage on new ones to meet her goals for net-new accounts, but only one and a half times the quota coverage was needed to meet those goals with her current customer base. This "land and expand" sales strategy was efficient and supported retention.

Growing with current customers is a strategy many leaders overlook. Many business leaders do not invest enough in customer success or growing their revenue from their current client base.

However, retaining a current client is always more cost effective and profitable than rebuilding a relationship from scratch. Any good university-level business program will teach you that in your first semester.

The key to connecting creative ideas to problems solving is to think as a solution-person rather than a selling-person. Consider more than just your perspective. How does your new idea impact your implementer and your customer? Think about outcomes. Consider the three primary drivers of modern business: people, process, and technology. You have to be creative and innovative around each of these tenets to even have a chance of building a successful cloud software business today.

True creative problem-solving often means doing what is right, not what is easy. Inertia is powerful and people will often hold on to "we've always done it this way" without thinking of ways to improve processes. Remember: your partners and team members are not always right. Even your customer is not always right. Creativity in sales requires having the confidence to make bold suggestions that may run up against the status quo.

Voynick believes that focusing on relationships and getting creative about how to care for your customer base is what sets you apart as a salesperson and leader. One of Voynick's long-time customers worked in the pharmaceutical industry and bought from Voynick as she moved from SAP to Ariba, and onward. He bought from her regardless of her employer because he liked the way Voynick solved his problems and that mattered more to him than the product itself.

At the end of the day, Voynick has learned that you want to be known for making things right, doing the right thing, and focusing on creatively addressing your customer's challenges. She advises that you want references that will say good things about you when asked, "what did they do when things went wrong?" When you navigate challenges with a customer and you do the right thing, you build incredible trust.

The trust that comes from the ability to problem solve on the fly pays dividends in good and bad times alike. Voynick was selling banking software in 2008. The day her employer planned to close the merger with Allscripts, Lehman Brothers filed bankruptcy. Lehman was the lead syndicator on the transaction. The Misys CEO assigned Voynick the task of maintaining sales and profits at target globally while he focused on securing alternative funding.

It was also up to Voynick to ensure that sales did not tank during these hard times. However, almost everything about their product had to change to succeed. Because Voynick and her team got creative and learned how other companies were pivoting, she too was able to pivot and make their product offerings fit company's operating budgets rather than CapEx . Due to Voynick's ability to innovate, the company stayed on plan.

In another example, Voynick joined a firm as a key sales and operations executive. The customer base was experiencing critical product issues. A forum of major customers met with her in her first week. They welcomed her and informed her she had 30 days to resolve the situation or they were pursuing a class action suit. Voynick decided to set up a program of regularly scheduled meetings and define what needed to be fixed.

She could not address all of their demands at once, but she was honest about what she could get done and they picked a few priorities every quarter to fix. They continued this process for several years. Her customers did not like when she said she could not do something that they were demanding, but she was transparent and realistic and helped them understand the process. It may not be what you think of as creative, but strong problem solving and realism about constraints are major factors in creativity. The meetings transitioned into positive customer advisory forums.

Now, Voynick spends most of her time as a member of many prominent boards and as an executive coach. As you would imagine, she is always trying to get her organizations to start thinking outside of the box in a way that drives innovation. She reminds them that great businesses are built by ensuring significant increases in business value driven by the right balance of investments and focus on people, processes, and technologies. That approach is no different than building a territory as a brand-new sales rep. If you aspire to become a sales or company leader, don't forget to start by being the CEO of your territory.

TITAN TIPS:

- Selling is a team sport and, as the account executive, you are the quarterback of the deal. Be respectful and get to know the talent across all functions of your organization. Everyone is in sales since nothing happens until we sell something.

- Creativity comes from many sources. You never know who might have a creative solution or be connected to the prospect organization.

- Make sure you have a solid customer value proposition that resonates through the prospect project team AND their executives. Is the solution focused on efficiency (making/ doing something better, cheaper, faster) or possibly a market innovation that can provide them a competitive advantage?

It is always helpful to understand the CEO's strategy and key initiatives. How does your solution support his/her agenda?

- Involve the prospect in each stage of the sales process. Don't exit a phase unless you and your prospect are aligned. How many times have we heard a deal is ready for a signature just to find the prospect is two steps behind the overly optimistic salesperson?

- There should always be a "give" and a "get" in a deal. Don't let a prospect send you on a journey of endless requests. Anytime the prospect requests something additional (another meeting, customer reference, etc.), ensure you "get" something in return to move the deal forward. Perhaps you arrange an additional customer reference in return for the opportunity for your execs to meet with theirs. Be clever in how you handle the "give and get" to ensure your prospect feels good about it.

- Creativity comes in many forms! Explore them all as you put your game plan together!

#6	# RESILIENCE
	### EMBRACING AND LEARNING FROM MISSTEPS TO BECOME A BETTER SALESPERSON

"A bend in the road isn't the end of the road unless you fail to make the turn."

- Helen Keller

Rejection and adversity are commonplace in sales. We get knocked down and we get up again. Again, and again, and again. Most people in sales will hear "no" more than "yes." You will be stood up and ignored, it's true, but behind each closed door is a priceless lesson—the sales greats are those that take the time to pause, reflect, and actually absorb and apply those lessons.

When we are faced with a difficult situation, we show our true colors. Those who respond to difficulty with resilience are well suited for a career in sales. Responding with resilience is a characteristic you can build up over time with practice. The key is to master your mindset.

To perfect the art of sales is to channel the art of resilience. In this chapter we will share strategies to overcome adversity, avoid focusing on closing, and dissect every deal in such a way that it will help win future deals.

OVERCOMING ADVERSITY

"While salespeople will find success when they lead with empathy, they'll find greater success when they respond with resilience."

- Gary Galvin, CEO Of Galvin Technologies

Since the sales world knocks us down repeatedly, those who succeed are resilient. Fortunately, our mindset has a great deal of power over how we react to adversity. The important thing is to remember that rejection does not mean you are worthless. Failure always hurts, but it is not permanent. The key to resilience is considering every loss an opportunity to learn and grow.

Next time something doesn't go your way, ask yourself these questions to reset your mindset:

1. What can I learn from this loss/failure/negative experience?

2. What can I do differently next time?

In addition to taking failure as an opportunity to learn, it's also important to remain calm and take responsibility for the role you played in the failure. This requires patience, self-awareness, and confidence, and it may be something you need to work toward over time.

Another great way to become more resilient is to spend time around resilient people. Jim Rohn famously said, "we are the average of the five people we spend the most time with." So, to succeed in sales, surround yourself with people who inspire you. They will give you courage, patience, perspective, and confidence to consider every negative experience an opportunity to learn.

TAKE "NO" FOR AN ANSWER

We discussed the value of taking no for an answer in the authenticity chapter. It applies to resilience too. "No" is not a word we like to hear often. Whether we are asking someone out to dinner or pitching a deal, "No" is not the answer we want to hear in our personal lives or professional lives.

Unfortunately, an anti-no culture has become so prevalent in sales and the primary focus of countless sales training programs. In fact—one of the basic belief systems in selling is, "Don't take 'no' for an answer." Now ask yourself, honestly—how do you feel when you say "no" to someone who will not take "no" for an answer? No one wants to be strong-armed into something they do not want or need. Not taking "no" for an answer is not a basis for effective selling.

Yet at this moment, a sales training class somewhere in the world is teaching sales professionals to never take "no" for an answer. There is a smooth, well-polished instructor in Milwaukee, Wisconsin, or Bangalore, India responding to possible objections with creative ways to keep the decision process alive.

This is not new; this is how the art of sales has been taught for many years. "Great sales professionals never take 'no' for an answer," the books say. They outline tactics for handling objections, reframing questions, changing the subject, presumptive closes, and so on ad infinitum.

Successful sales leaders like Andrew Fritts, SVP Global Sales at N3 have been doing this right for years. Andrew likes the word "no." Why? He views it as an opportunity to learn what a client really wants, and in most cases, what they need to be successful. It's one of the reasons he has personally sold over $150M in SaaS and services over his career.

Andrew was originally trained in product marketing. His strategic approach to his sales career evolved over time, but it was always rooted in knowing the client's needs and tailoring the partnership models accordingly. He learned quickly that there is value in hearing "no" early. "No" gave him the opportunity to pivot and re-tailor the solution he provided to the specific relationship's needs. Or, it gave him the opportunity to thank prospects for their time and sharpen his persona targeting going forward. In many cases, prospects were so grateful for his "non-salesy approach" that they were more flexible themselves.

The fact that not trying to force the client to accept a different reality is viewed as "non-salesy" is the core problem. The market believes that salespeople are out to convince them of things with which they disagree. When salespeople like Andrew change the language and tone of the conversation, prospects are pleasantly surprised by the level of authenticity, so much so that they go out of their way to find ways to work with him.

Let's be clear: the implicit objective in such approaches to selling—which is to say, most selling as usually taught—is to get the customer to do what the seller wants, even if it is not what the customer wants. That is not Andrew's approach.

If you operate from the belief system that the object of selling is to get the customer to do what the seller wants, even if it is not what the customer wants, you are setting yourself up for disappointment. If you hold an inner belief that a salesperson is "justified" and "deserving" of a sale, you are destined to feel resentment and anger when it doesn't happen.

As humans, we all feel disappointment at a lost sale. As evolved sales professionals, we don't let it turn to anger and resentment. We need a sales ethos that argues the same thing. We need a system of selling in which the objective of selling is to get the customer what the customer wants.

So, if a good salesperson is not someone who can turn a "no" into a "yes"—then what is a good salesperson? It is very simple: a good salesperson is one that knows early on when a "no" is a "no," and focuses his or her efforts on the leads that promise a potential "yes."

It turns out "no" is not such a terrible word. It teaches us a great deal. Accepting "no" can help train us to become the type of salesperson we want to be: a salesperson with integrity, honesty, and truly productive relationships with clients.

Accepting "no" over the course of a career also allows us to hit our full revenue production potential because it frees up more room for clients who are better fits.

So, try accepting a "no" and see if it gets you a few more shots at "yes" down the road.

DON'T FOCUS ON CLOSING

In many industries, being dubbed a "closer" is the highest accolade a sales professional can achieve. The term encapsulates the skills and traits necessary to become a top-level performer. Closers are the most highly recruited and sought after—the true elite. However, most of us don't even like to be considered salespeople— much less closers!

This is a true statement despite the fact that we can close with the best of them and that many Cloud Software executives consider closing important. Many a senior partner or CEO has said, "if we only had someone who can close around here we'd have a lot more business." But the reality is, sales close themselves if they've been worked properly throughout the sales process.

HERE'S A STORY TO ILLUSTRATE THE POINT:

Jim Campbell is a prominent real estate developer in Tucson, Arizona. From the 1980s to the early 2000s, Campbell was the President and co-founder of The Application Group (AG), the first PeopleSoft consulting partner. He is the kind of special leader people naturally learn from, beginning the day they meet him.

The first time Mark met Campbell; it was during Mark's final interview for The Application Group —his first choice to begin his consulting selling career after a few years as a strategy consultant. He remembers thinking, "This is where I close the deal."

But as Mark walked into Campbell's office, he noticed small white notes everywhere all with the phrase, "Never, Ever Close" written on them. Mark had already been told that his interview with Campbell would be complex and challenging. On top of that, it was Mark's closing sales meeting, and here were notes telling Mark he was exactly wrong.

Was this a psychological gambit to throw him off-guard? Did Campbell actually mean it? How could Mark leverage his newly minted Marketing/Sales focused MBA in this discussion when everything he learned in school screamed "no!" to these words?

Mark quickly learned why Campbell worked so hard to remind himself and his team of this belief. Campbell—an engineer by training, not a salesperson—never sold in a conventional sales process way. Though he was in a marketplace that constantly focused on sales processes and closing methodologies, he found success via a different route: being himself.

Campbell values his business relationships deeply. Each one of them is based on an unrelenting level of trust and respect. He cares about every one of his clients and business partners. He is a consummate builder of relationships founded on principles of trust. This ensured his success in enterprise software consulting and throughout his real estate development career.

"In sales, being a hard worker helps, but you need to think beyond that. Stay current and relevant to what's important to your prospects. Believe that you can succeed no matter how many deals you lose. Get up, brush yourself off, and move on. Most importantly, focus on what matters to your customers before you think about your comp plan."

- Maria Pulsoni-Cicio, Strategic Account Manager at Informatica

BECOME MORE TRUSTED AND RESPECTED, SELL MORE

How did Campbell earn this reputation? He is the kind of person who loves life, has deep spiritual beliefs, and has the philosopher's knack for reflection and insight about relationships.

Campbell's inclination and intimate concern for his clients' well-being translate naturally into trust-based relationships. His clients genuinely desire to see his business grow. They give Campbell business whenever they can and they refer to him within their network. Campbell has discovered that when you bring this kind of belief system to a sales process, you don't have to close to win.

Campbell's approach works better in some industries and sales environments than others. Buying a car, for example, is a process so encrusted with ancient roles and expectations that every seller knows to move quickly toward closing, and every buyer knows to expect it. But the following characteristics are situation where Campbell's approach works best:

- Complex sales
- Intangible services/complicated physical products

- Long-term relationships

- High risk and high return

- High degrees of technical competence required by seller

Do any of these situations sound familiar to you? If so, you are likely in the enviable position of never needing to close. Some examples of industries that fit these descriptions include computer hardware, heavy equipment, aircraft, software, accounting, legal, industrials and many other B2B industries.

Professional buyers—no matter how good the selling is—will buy when (and only when) it is appropriate for them to buy. There is no impulse or pressure buying occurring at Google, Microsoft, Pfizer, or Goldman Sachs. At the same time, it is a myth that they buy solely on rational criteria; issues like the integrity of the salesperson are critical. All buying decisions are, at least in part, emotional.

HOW DO YOU WIN WITHOUT EVER CLOSING?

The process of closing uses up a great deal of "Trust Capital." Trust Capital is what you generate throughout the sales cycle that will allow you to win. The one with the most trust equity generated on decision day wins the deal, not the one who burns the most. And that right there is the problem with the traditional approach to "closing." It is focused on short-term, selfishly defined objectives. In any larger sense, it isn't winning at all.

Some small part of Trust Capital is based on external factors, many of which you do not directly control. In most cases, you can only affect the perception of things like product quality, your firm's reputation, and risk associated with your product or service.

However, Trust Capital is also significantly affected by every act, comment, and message (or lack thereof) you deliver. Your behavior is your responsibility and yours only. Like a solid product design, it matters a great deal which characteristics you begin with and how you develop them throughout your lifetime. Integrity and other personal virtues we often consider too "soft" to be meaningful are in fact tremendously powerful forces in sales success.

These intrinsic personal capabilities (IPCs) are what allowed Campbell to become one of the most renowned business developers in the application software and consulting marketplace. He knows that the way he is perceived affects his success ratio. He also knows that the level of consideration and respect he gives his clients translates into more business for him as a consulting professional.

True success is not about having the best sales methodology or always saying the right thing at the right time. It is about continuously and steadfastly building your own IPCs.

Campbell believes that trust is lost when pressuring a prospect into a close. He instead finalizes a sale by ensuring that every question that could be asked by the prospect is answered and every step of the decision process is fulfilled. He does so naturally, out of an outgrowth of his IPCs, because he is focused on total client satisfaction. By conducting his affairs in that way, he doesn't have to "close" in the way we traditionally think of that term. Instead, the close occurs naturally.

Campbell has learned that he never, ever has to close. You don't have to, either.

LEARN FROM EVERY DEAL

Every deal, whether it is won or lost, is worth dissecting and learning from. Strong sales organizations build a process around this. Lost deals are not all bad. In fact, you learn a lot more from lost deals than won deals. In our experience, the best sales deal reviews are not done in a vacuum. Instead, they are done with a team. At Anaplan, Paul started a presentation series called "The Anatomy of a Deal" in which a sales rep would give a presentation about a great win or a tough loss in front of the entire company. It was a vulnerable task, but incredibly helpful to the sales rep and to the entire organization. In the presentation, the salesperson would review what could be done better. Ultimately, the process became a great sales enablement tool and an opportunity for company-wide engagement.

THERE'S NO SUCH THING AS CLOSING

Let us take this a step further. Let's pause and consider whether closing even exists.

If you think of closing as the sole purpose of your sales process, this thought probably seems ludicrous to you. However, we encourage you to consider the idea that closing is not your sole goal. Think of closing as a non-thing, just the last step in a process called "selling" that is largely intangible. Realize that making "the sale" is an artificial mental construct.

The reality is, as salespeople, we have a pretty simple job. We have ongoing conversations with potential buyers. Periodically, those conversations trigger a commercial event: first the buyer signs a contract, then the seller receives payment. Our market capitalist system links those two events. Yes, the absence of any such commercial events would ultimately render the relationship unsustainable for both parties. However, as long as there are occasional commercial events sufficient to sustain an ongoing relationship, the dialogue we call "sales" continues.

In our SaaS world, how many times do we think we have "closed" a deal only to later learn that we never really did? One distinct example of this is when a deal is closed and then in twelve months lose the renewal, or sometimes, depending on the contract terms, much sooner.

The bulk of sales is the dialogue and interaction, and we believe the most successful salespeople are those who focus on leveraging that dialogue and interaction to help their customers, not sell them. That is the essence of effective selling.

The commercial event—the sale—is grossly over-celebrated. In reality, the "sale" is simply one event among many equally important events. Each commercial event, lost or won, is not unlike the hundreds of "nos" and dozens of "yeses" we hear on an ongoing basis in all of our relationships.

The only reason to track "closed" sales is to generally know if we are getting it right (i.e., are we getting better at this or worse over time). Tracking sales helps us understand if there are trends affecting our ability to impact our clients' businesses and if the general marketplace is supporting or hindering us.

After years in sales, we no longer think about a sale, much less a closing or a "no." We are not suggesting that sales is not a process or that methodologies are a bad thing, but the process of selling when done by the best of us is a circular or continuous one, not a linear finite one.

Further, we are suggesting, particularly in the SaaS world, we take a more holistic view of our sales results rather than attaching to and celebrating individual deals. Basically, by embracing the philosophy that if you have an effective process rooted in keeping the dialogue going and keeping your client's best interests in mind, enough of those conversations will trigger commercial events that keep the doors open.

CHAPTER TAKEAWAYS

VIEW ADVERSITY AS A LEARNING OPPORTUNITY

Failure always hurts, but it is not permanent. The key to resilience is taking every loss as an opportunity to learn and grow.

TIPS FOR LEARNING FROM ADVERSITY:

- Ask yourself: what can I learn from this loss/failure/negative experience?

- Ask yourself: what can I do differently next time?

- Surround yourself with resilient people who inspire you.

- Dissect every deal. Whether it is won or lost, discuss with your team the reasons why you succeeded or failed and apply the lessons to future deals.

DON'T BE AFRAID TO TAKE "NO" FOR AN ANSWER

A good salesperson is not someone who can turn a "no" into a "yes." A good salesperson is one that knows early on when a "no" is a "no," and focuses his or her efforts on the leads that promise a potential "yes."

TIPS FOR KNOWING WHEN TO TAKE "NO" FOR AN ANSWER:

- Focus on what the customer truly needs. Remember your goal should always be to give the customer something they want, not what you want.

- Don't force, adapt. If you are forcing what you want on the customer, adapt your solution or walk away.

- Remember a "no" frees up time and resources for better opportunities. Keep your pipeline full of quality opportunities so that you can turn away prospects that are not good fits.

CLOUD TITAN:
GREG HOLMES, FORMER CHIEF STRATEGY
OFFICER AT ZOOM, BOARD MEMBER AT
CHORUS.AI

From House Painter and Teacher to Technology Game Changer: Learning and Leading Along the Way

ABOUT GREG

Greg Holmes has more than a decade of experience in sales and management in the SaaS space. Most recently, he served as Chief Strategy Officer and Chief Revenue Officer at Zoom Video Communications. His storied career brought him from school teaching to early leadership positions at CA Technologies within the Nimsoft product division. He helped build the web touch selling model at Webex, and successfully ran the Canadian business unit for Cisco Webex, where he grew revenues from $2M to $12M in his two years leading the team. Greg is a graduate of the University of California, Santa Barbara.

Greg Holmes understands the power of resilience. To hear him tell it, resilience is really about simply showing up and doing your best no matter where you are in life or what you are faced with. It is this philosophy that propelled Holmes into leadership positions in every job he has held, including CRO at one of the largest ever SaaS success stories.

Holmes grew up in Northern California and faced adversity early on in his life. He grew up with parents who struggled with alcoholism and he learned very early in life that he needed to focus and drive forward every day to break free. Through this journey, and many more hurdles he faced along the way, he learned that when you put your head down and work hard, you can accomplish incredible things.

Hard work paired with true resilience is what put Holmes on a fast (albeit winding and bumpy) track to software titan status. True resilience is not just about being strong, it's about being flexible, embracing change, and learning from adversity, rather than buckling under its weight and throwing up your hands

Holmes has been a 2nd and 4th grade teacher, a sport's coach, and a painting contractor. His close proximity to Silicon Valley and the dot com boom opened his mind to a career in technology innovation.

We are certain Holmes would have found a way to give back in immense ways whether he stuck with teaching, house painting, or any other profession he found a passion for. World changers change worlds no matter what, through whatever means they are presented with. And he's nowhere close to being done impacting our world, even after his recent decision to part from Zoom to spend more time with his family.

His technology career started at Webex after a teacher friend, who made a similar move, recommended he give it a try. Being an intuitive person, he found that much of what he'd learned as a teacher (managing personalities) and as a contractor (grit and hard work) applied directly to sales. Holmes' ability to intuit best practices, follow his gut, and think creatively got him promoted very quickly and often. He moved from leading the CSM team to operations leadership, to leading WebEx's Canadian business development unit. His ideas took WebEx's Canadian business unit from $3 million in revenue to $25 million within three years.

During his time at WebEx, he worked with the CEO of Zoom. The CEO remembered him and sent him a LinkedIn message when they had a sales position opening. Holmes' willingness to be open to change allowed him to take the leap to Zoom, a small company at the time. He was given a blank canvas: build a sales team.

Part of what attracted Holmes to Zoom was its culture. That culture was based on a simple idea: deliver happiness. That meant listening, caring, and not making it about the deal. That philosophy is what separated Zoom from competitors at the time. They won deals because people actually liked to interact with their sales team. Doing the right thing was the priority, and it paid off.

The company also prioritized giving people responsibility and purpose beyond sales (like volunteering or arranging a social event for the team). They found that this approach expands the person as an individual and builds structure and harmony amongst the team.

The biggest lesson Holmes has gathered in all of his leadership positions is this: take today and be the best at whatever you are doing today. Move the process forward. You do not have to close the deal every day. Some days will be rougher than others. Setbacks will come. You will be asked to do things that are outside of your job description. Keep doing the work, move the process forward, and opportunities will open up to you.

TITAN TIPS:

- Don't be afraid to think outside of the scope of your job description. This means thinking beyond your to-do list and focusing on delivering happiness to your clients. It's never about the deal. It's always about listening and truly caring about your prospect's experience.

- Move something forward each day. Success in sales is all about continuing to do the work, day after day, and making moves toward your goals, even if they are small moves.

- Always act with pure intentions. When you act with pure intentions, opportunities will present themselves.

#7 | TRUST

A SUCCESSFUL SALES CAREER IS BUILT ON TRUST-FILLED RELATIONSHIPS

"When trust is present, things go more quickly and cost less. When trust is absent, things go more slowly and cost more."

- Stephen MR Covey Jr.

As consumers, we understand the influence of someone we trust. When you make an investment, where do you look for guidance? Commonly, we ask trusted advisors, colleagues, family, and friends for recommendations. Beyond that, we look for third-party validation through things like rankings, reviews, and forums. We have more information at our fingertips than ever. In fact, Gartner research found that today's customers are 57% of the way through the purchase process before they have the first meaningful contact with a seller. That is why we must deliver a purchase experience that transcends product features and benefits.

Consider this—are you more likely to make a sale when you: a) show up as a stranger with flyers and bullet points, or b) already have a relationship with a prospect and bring good questions and engaging stories with your customer in mind?

The clear answer is "b." Flyers and bullet points position you as a salesperson. Good questions and stories position you as a resource. To build the meaningful strategic alliances and partnerships necessary to succeed in software sales, you need to focus on being a resource, not a salesperson. This requires earning and maintaining trust, nurturing intimacy-based relationships, and logging meaningful face time with prospects, colleagues, and partners.

"Sales organizations can increase business by challenging customers — delivering customer interactions specifically designed to disrupt their current thinking and teach them something new. It's not just about selling something anymore." Brent Adamson, Distinguished Vice President, Advisory, Gartner and co-author of The Challenger Sale, Taking Control of the Customer Conversation

The bottom line is this: when your customers and partners do not trust you, they will not buy from you, partner with you, or refer you for new opportunities. When they trust you, you will experience a faster sales cycle and a more sustainable and fruitful relationship. In this chapter, we outline how to build trust and intimacy to yield more profitable relationships.

EARNING AND MAINTAINING TRUST

Earning trust requires that you be consistently authentic, discreet, caring, reliable, and credible. Your goal is to work toward a relationship with your customer and strategic alliances in which your customers let go of the fear of being "sold" and, instead, turn to you for advice and expertise.

Someone who trusts you knows that you have their best interest in mind. You can build trust over time by always doing what you say you are going to do and going out of your way to provide value to your prospects, customers, and partners. Your prospects must believe that you are genuine and honest. They must feel comfortable sharing information with you, and they must feel that you care. The most successful salespeople earn trust by being genuine, honest, and truly caring about prospects and partners.

It is important that you consistently show up with every interaction and every result you deliver. Remember, little inconsistencies add up. According to Heiman Miller's Conceptual Selling, lack of trust is the reason 60% of sales fail. That is more than any other reason combined, including a lack of need, desire, urgency, or budget.

Building Lasting Intimacy-Based Relationships

Increasingly, software sales are about relationships. As we have outlined, meaningful and productive relationships require a certain level of trust and intimacy. Business intimacy may sound inappropriate, but trust us, it's not as risqué as it sounds. Some may take exception to the notion of integrating emotions into business, but the reality is buying decisions are emotional.

People are bombarded with choices of products and services. Let's be honest, your product or service is good, but then so are most of your competitors. You know it, your company knows it, and, oftentimes, so does the consumer. What makes the difference, and creates our personal success, is the ability to build and nurture relationships through conscious effort.

There is a quote from the movie "The Godfather," "Don't think of this as personal, it's only business." Right after this statement, the mobster proceeds to murder the individual. Murder is about as personal as it can get. Business and personal are completely intertwined, no matter how hard you try to keep them separate.

It is a bit of a conundrum, isn't it? Salespeople do not have the best track record in personal and family relationships, and yet our retirement income depends on our ability to relate to others through trust and business intimacy.

Transcending these layers requires that you be willing to ask tough questions and get vulnerable with your prospects. If you will not

INTIMACY-BASED RELATIONSHIPS

communicate authentically on a personal level, neither will your prospects.

Every conversation you have with any individual is contributing to that relationship, whether a good one or not. The comments you make to the gas station attendant, the tip you leave the waitress at your favorite lunch spot, the notes you send to your secretary, or the email you quickly draft to a new client all become another thread in the tenuous connection we call a relationship.

HERE IS A PERSONAL STORY TO ILLUSTRATE THE IMPORTANCE OF BUILDING TRUST AND ESTABLISHING AN INTIMACY-BASED RELATIONSHIP:

Mark's daughter, Mirabella, was a premature baby in the NICU for three weeks and was fighting sepsis. An amazing team of providers were tasked with working all day and night to ensure she survived. At the center of that team was Dr. Wang, a first- or second-year doctor. Rather than consulting only with his team, he involved

Mark and his wife, Michelle, in the decision process of caring for Mirabella. There were multiple scenarios and it was not black and white. He brought them to a back room of the hospital and wrote up the different scenarios and the pros and cons on a whiteboard. He built trust with them by being vulnerable and letting them into his process of analyzing exactly where Mirabella was medically and how to fight the sepsis. The two primary options were to use a typical antibiotic or an aggressive new antibiotic. By involving Michelle and Mark, Dr. Wang transcended from a director-type role to an advisor. Dr. Wang was performing a service rather than a transaction. Ultimately, they decided as a team to pursue the aggressive IV antibiotic. Within a few hours, Mirabella was off the ventilator and color returned to her face. She is now a healthy, happy, beautiful, and brilliant 16 year old.

What saved Mark's daughter's life? Was it the love of her parents, the medical technology, prayer support, or the vast experience of the physician? Of course, all of these contributed to her survival, but if they had not taken the time to know and trust the physician, and if Dr. Wang had been routine and limited to the function of his duties, it's uncertain whether the correct decision would have been made in time.

When your conversations start from a place of trust, every communication you have is more effective and actionable. You start a level deeper than you do with non-intimate business relationships, which expedites your ability to get to the heart of the matter and provide a meaningful solution. When you have intimacy with your customer, they are much more likely to carefully consider your recommendations and recommend you to others.

It is important to note, you will not achieve intimacy with every prospect and customer, and that is OK. The most trust-filled relationships require chemistry, time, and countless interactions. They do not bloom overnight or after one dinner or golf outing. They require showing up meeting after meeting, call after call, and event after event, and earning trust over time.

WHAT TO DO IF TRUST IS VIOLATED

No one is perfect, and there will be times in your sales career where you are not able to deliver what you promised. When this happens, owning your mistakes and being honest is a great way to earn trust.

SIX STEPS TO TAKE AFTER TRUST VIOLATION

1. Acknowledge. Acknowledge that you have not delivered what you promised.

2. Address Feelings. Take time to express that you understand any emotional impact your misstep may have made on the other party.

3. Get Support. Ask for help or delegate. Often, we miss marks because we take on too much. Don't be afraid to ask questions to your clients, partners, and colleagues along the way.

4. Take Responsibility for Your Part. One of the most surefire ways to lose respect and trust is to blame your mistakes on others. Always, always, always own your role.

5. Appreciate Forgiveness. Acknowledge and express gratitude for the other party's patience and forgiveness.

6. Move on and Learn. Don't carry your mistakes around with you. Instead, consider what you can learn from the mistake and try to apply that lesson in the future.

Let's face it, relationships are not easy. If they were, a whole host of folks would be out of a job, even Dr. Phil! We depend on journalists, psychiatrists, psychologists, therapists, counselors, friends, family, and even reality TV (well, maybe not) to tell us how to navigate human relationships.

THE POWER OF FACE TIME

We live in an era filled with digital distractions. The temptation to skip in-person meetings is strong with texting, social media, email, video-conferencing—you name it. These tools do save time and money, and enable us to engage in a way we've never been able to before, but they don't move the needle the way face time does.

Planning a dinner or grabbing a cup of coffee goes a long way. According to research by a UCLA professor Dr. Albert Mehrabian, 55% of communication is visual, not verbal. Research also shows that in-person conversations tend to be more positive and perceived as more credible than online conversations.

Think about your best clients. Does that list correlate with the clients you see most frequently face-to-face? It's likely that it does, because meeting in person helps build business intimacy. In person you can read body language, bond in a more meaningful way, and think on a more complex level. According to Harvard Business Review, 95% of those polled said that face-to-face meetings are crucial to "building and maintaining long term relationships," and 88% believed that successful sales depend on face time.

Meeting face-to-face gives you the opportunity to develop trust through business conversations. When you make a connection, listen actively, understand needs, and jointly brainstorm solutions with your prospects, partners, or colleagues. You are much more likely to close a sale through making a connection than with cold calling or emailing.

If you think about your most successful business deals, we bet money that human-to-human, face-to-face, high-touch communication has repeatedly played a role in that and accelerated your sales cycle over and over.

This advice goes beyond making connections with prospects and customers. It is just as important with colleagues. Face time is just as invaluable with prospects as it is with your team. As sales teams are increasingly dispersed, it's more important than ever to consciously make time to connect with colleagues. This is especially important if you have team members from different countries and cultures. It is impossible to span cultural differences and build deep and lasting trust without periodically bringing people together in person.

However, we are now in the COVID-19 pandemic era and hopefully soon, the post COVID-19 era once medical technology brings this virus into a less than global pandemic state. So, until we meet (face-to-face) again...

INVOKING ALL FIVE SENSES EVEN WHEN YOU'RE NOT IN-PERSON - HOW TO BE A VIRTUAL TRUSTED ADVISOR

In the last section, we emphasized the importance of face time—and we mean face time, not FaceTime. However, the reality is you will not always have the opportunity or bandwidth to get face-to-face with your prospect. The good news is you can invoke some of the same benefits virtually.

Every human being is hardwired to assess the people they interact with on multiple levels—mental, physical, emotional, and subconscious. As you sell, there will be times when you click with a prospect on multiple levels. A good way to connect with prospects is to be cognizant of how you are affecting all five of their senses: touch, taste, sight, smell, and sound. Good sales organizations engage all five senses during face-to-face meetings. Great salespeople strive to invoke as many senses as possible, even when the meeting is not in person.

Regardless of the bandwidth of the channel of communication you are dealing with, you should strive to invoke as many of the senses as deeply as you can. So, for example:

- Get photos on your website and LinkedIn page.

- Make a specific comment on the background of the person you're talking to on video chat. It shows you're interested and makes a connection, even if only in a small way.

- Always use your own camera on video chat (and get the lighting and the audio right). A weak camera six inches from your face on a laptop will not work for you especially if, like us, you don't look like Beyoncé or Ryan Reynolds.

- When on audio-only calls, have the person's picture in front of you; if you don't have their photo, go to LinkedIn and get it. Put it on your "Notes" page while you talk to them (in direct sales, the admonition is "smile before you dial" because people can intuit it).

- Look up the weather in the prospect's city before you call; comment on it early on and decide if you want to share that it's 75 and sunny in your hometown of San Diego or Miami.

- As Charlie Green, author of "Trusted Advisor" and "Trust-

Based Selling" shares often on his blog, bring (or send) a risky gift (B.A.R.G.) The more specific to the receiver, the better. Use every bit of knowledge you have and can ascertain to give a gift that shows you have been paying attention. The riskier the gift, the more you show you trust the receiver enough to risk totally missing the mark. An example would be going out of the way to find a Scotch Whiskey that was distilled nearby to where your client recently went on a golf holiday, but then find out she or he gave up alcohol completely two years ago. Even a miscalculation like this will most often build, not diminish trust and intimacy.

- Perform as many virtual gracious acts as you can. In simple terms it is really just about ensuring, especially when you are interacting virtually that you have interest in them as a person, not just someone who will help you get to Club this year. It can be as simple as asking about how a client's child is doing in a new school or how their spouse's golf game is progressing.

Face time is an ideal way to engage, but there are many options available to us through technology. Face time includes a lot of flying-time or windshield-time, neither is fun in large doses.

Zoom, WebEx, Microsoft Teams, and a host of others are great alternatives to the productivity involved in travel. After many years of struggle, many (especially tech-focused) companies are getting really good at leveraging their video conferencing tools. COVID-19 accelerated adoption of this model. Even laggards to this model, like old-school sales professionals like us, are embracing video conferencing as an effective alternative to travel. Although it may seem like a drag to up your wardrobe game when you are not traveling (make sure to shave and skip the baseball cap), video calls allow you to connect on a much more meaningful level with prospects than a phone call alone.

Next time you set up a meeting, consider how you can level-up the way you engage. For example, if you were going to send an email, can you call instead? Or, if you were planning to call by phone, can you make it a video call? Every level-up matters.

CHAPTER TAKEAWAYS

EARNING TRUST REQUIRES CONSISTENT AUTHENTICITY

Your goal is to work toward a relationship with your customer and strategic alliances in which they let go of the fear of being "sold" and instead turn to you for advice and expertise. Someone who trusts you knows that you have their best interest in mind.

TIPS FOR EARNING TRUST THROUGH AUTHENTICITY

- Do what you say you are going to do. You can build trust over time by always doing what you say you're going to do. You earn trust every day through every interaction you have and every result you deliver.

- Always be honest. Little inconsistencies add up to broken trust, and broken trust has a cost. According to Heiman Miller's Conceptual Selling, lack of trust is the reason 60% of sales fail. That's more than any other reason combined, including lack of need, desire, urgency, or budget.

OWN TRUST VIOLATIONS

No one is perfect, and there will be times in your sales career where you are not able to deliver what you promised. When this happens, owning your mistakes and being honest is a great way to earn trust:

WHAT TO DO AFTER A TRUST VIOLATION:

1. Acknowledge: Acknowledge that you haven't delivered what you promised.

2. Address the Feelings: Take time to express that you understand any emotional impact your misstep may have made on the other party.

3. Get Support: Ask for help or delegate. Often, we miss marks because we take on too much. Don't be afraid to ask questions of your clients, partners, and colleagues along the way.

4. Take Responsibility for Your Part: One of the most surefire ways to lose respect and trust is to blame your mistakes on others. Always, always, always own your role.

5. Appreciate Forgiveness: Acknowledge and express gratitude for the other party's patience and forgiveness.

6. Move on and Learn: Don't carry your mistakes around with you. Instead, consider what you can learn from every mistake and try to apply that lesson in the future.

BUILDING LASTING INTIMACY-BASED RELATIONSHIPS

People are bombarded with choices of products and services. Let's be honest, your product or service is good, but then, so are most of your competitors. You know it, your company knows it, and oftentimes so does the consumer. What makes the difference and creates our personal success, is our ability to build and nurture relationships through conscious effort.

TIPS FOR CULTIVATING INTIMACY-BASED RELATIONSHIPS:

1. Loosen the barrier between business and personal. Business and personal are completely intertwined, no matter how

hard you try to keep them separate. To achieve the highest level of partnership with our customers and prospects, we must transcend from data-based relationships to intimacy-based (or emotion-based) relationships.

2. Intuit your prospect's challenges. Take time to understand the professional and personal impact that challenge presents, offer a solution to their challenge, and deliver on that solution.

3. Ask tough questions and be vulnerable. If you do not communicate authentically on a personal level, neither will your prospects.

4. Build deep, long-lasting relationships through whatever enablers you have at your disposal, virtual or in-person, when possible. For example, build trusted business relationships like Warren Wirth. Warren is a senior business development executive at Kronos/Ultimate Software who is successful because he nurtures, protects and cherishes his business relationships in the same exact way he does his personal ones. Mark knows this because he has both a long-term business relationship and friendship with Warren. Remember all business is personal, and that resonates more than anything.

CLOUD TITAN
CHARLES GREEN, AUTHOR,
SPEAKER, CONSULTANT
FOUNDER OF TRUSTEDADVISOR.COM

The Power of Trust and Transparency in Sales

ABOUT CHARLIE
Charlie Green is a world renowned thought leader in trust-based

selling. He co-authored The Trusted Advisor and its follow-up The Trusted Advisor Fieldbook as well as Trust-Based Selling. For 20+ years, Charlie has traveled the world as a consultant, author, and speaker sharing his passion for trust-based selling and leadership. Charlie has helped hundreds of companies build models to ensure their employees interact with clients and prospects with more honesty, authenticity, and a focus on them, not us.

Fresh from completing his Philosophy degree at Columbia in 1972, Charlie found himself working in Washington D.C. during Nixon's impeachment. His time there put a spotlight on the damage that distrust can wreak on organizations especially the largest ones like governments. Even then, as a young man, he thought "there has to be a better way." He wanted to dedicate his career to helping organizations run better.

To learn more about how businesses run, he earned an MBA at Harvard Business School. After graduation, he landed a gig at a consulting firm. For 19+ years, Charlie consulted with a variety of businesses. He noticed one common thread along the way: success running a business effectively comes down to human relationships.

After two decades of consulting, Charlie was burnt out. Within a 4-month timespan, Charlie left his gig at the consulting firm, got divorced, quit drinking and met his second wife. When faced with this major pivot point in his life, something serendipitous happened. He attended a Deloitte training program that was bringing in well known business speakers and marketing consultants to work with their partners.. One speaker missed their flight and Charlie was asked to put together a presentation about being something called a "Trusted Advisor" within a half hour. That serendipitous happening sparked what would become 4 books and countless keynote speaking addresses.

Charlie began relentlessly researching the concept of being a trusted advisor. Eventually, he partnered with co-authors working on a book on a similar topic and found that the idea that trust drives company and sales success resonated deeply with many. Charlie was able to apply what he learned about client relationships from consulting, business from business school, emotional connection from the 12-step program, and critical thinking from his undergraduate degree to tap into the idea that we can achieve powerful things if we look at our businesses through the lens of trust-based relationships.

Trust-based relationships power business success. Period. This statement is especially true in the sales realm. Every sales person wants to make a difference and be genuine. No one wants to be a pushy salesman. Yet, we must at some point make sales to thrive in our economy. Trust-based selling helps reconcile this conflict. Despite what you may think, clients will reward you if they do not feel pushed or conned. Therefore, doing what is best for your client and focusing on doing what you say you are going to do to build trust will ultimately drive more sales for you than pushing someone into something they don't want or need.

HERE'S A STORY TO ILLUSTRATE THE POWER OF TRUST AND TRANSPARENCY:

There was a Senior VP Charlie worked with at the consulting firm who notoriously underbid projects. Charlie had been burned a few times. The two needed to work together to bid a project. Charlie told him the project could be no less than $120,000. They agreed. However, during the client meeting, the Senior VP told the client it would only be $90,000. Because Charlie knew he had built trust with the client he called the Senior VP out in the meeting in front of *the client. The Senior VP protested after the meeting, saying "you can't do that in front of a client." However, later that evening, the client called Charlie and said "you got the job and you got it at 120. It was clear to me you thought it through and I want your ass on the line with no excuses." This example shows that when you approach things with transparency and client focus, you win.*

When you are honest with your clients and prospects, you are more likely to win more clients that are better fits for your company. For example, if you bend the truth, spin the positioning or flat out lie about an issue your client cares about or agree with something your client says that does not align with your personal or professional values, the relationship is doomed down the road. Charlie preaches this: always speak the truth and don't be concerned about the win or the loss because trust-based relationships are inherently win-win.

HERE ARE SOME OF CHARLIE'S TOP TIPS TO BUILD TRUST:

- When you don't know something, say so: 95% of sales reps will make up an answer when asked a question to which they don't know the answer. That will backfire down the road. Instead of bluffing, say "I don't know that answer" and pause. Be forthright about declaring the limits of their knowledge. You will gain huge points for transparency.

- "Wow" is a full sentence: Every interaction is unique to the two people and the moment you are in. The more powerful conversations are emotional ones. If you have an emotional reaction in the moment, have it. It will show that you don't have another agenda and you are in the moment.

- The best way to short term performance is long term management: We think the more we break down data the better, but the opposite is true. It can be tough to shift to thinking about long term trust rather than short-term revenue. However, if you focus all your efforts on revenue, your clients will see through that. It's much more powerful to convey that your goal is to help them achieve their goals.

- You could be a better listener: Listen to validate and ensure your client knows they are being heard and you are devoted to them and nothing else. Bonus? Humans are hardwired to return the favor. If you genuinely listen to your customer, they are more likely to genuinely listen to you.

#8

TRUST-BASED GO-TO MARKET MODELS

LEARN THE SALES MODELS THAT THRIVE IN THE MODERN SALES ENVIRONMENT

"You can raise the bar or you can wait for others to raise it, but it's getting raised regardless."

- Seth Godin, Author and Speaker

We believe the three most powerful sales strategies in our space today are private equity go-to-market strategy, customer success, and consulting partnerships/strategic alliances. We explore each of these strategies in this chapter, but you can be sure about one thing: they all require an immense amount of trust. If there is one thing you focus on in your sales career, let it be a genuine commitment to building trust-based relationships rooted in good intentions, mutual benefit, and good-old-fashioned human-to-human interaction.

When your customers and strategic partners think of you as a trusted resource, they are more likely to take your advice to heart and have more constructive conversations with you. Trust enables intimacy, and it opens doors. The key is mastering the art of earning it.

Over the course of our careers, software sales has evolved significantly. Despite our different career paths, Mark and Paul have remained connected and kept in touch because of the evolution of common go-to-market models. We have both been involved early in the evolution of enterprise software selling approaches and were early adopters and in some cases creators of the innovative strategies that have made enterprise-level cloud software sales a holy grail of B2B selling.

Software sales executives are known for innovation because they are forever creating newfangled programs and initiatives. Early hardware and software executives devised strategies to partner up and sell to their prospects in concerted fashions, both internally and externally with groups such as consultancies, other hardware and software players, and Value-Added-Resellers (VARS). Many of these initiatives were successful because—of course—the more parties involved, the better the G2 (Competitive Information). However, although the information is useful, the process of partnering to sell is not always efficient.

Just as sales leaders before us have pioneered new approaches to sales, we have tried to do the same throughout our careers. Some have been unprecedented winners; others have fallen flat. In this chapter, we will focus on three leading software sales models we helped pioneer: private equity go-to-market, customer success, and consulting partnerships/strategic alliances. Each requires establishing and nurturing a loyal relationship based on business intimacy and genuine human connection.

THE STRATEGIC ALLIANCE ECOSYSTEM

We were both early adopters of the strategic alliance ecosystem pioneered by Klaus Besier (previous President and CEO of SAP America, Inc.) in the 80s. Besier is a titan of SaaS leadership and he is responsible for much of the rapid growth enterprise technology companies have experienced. He grew SAP from $50 million to $1 billion in revenue in less than 5 years. The approach is born from the idea that alliances gain more by sharing knowledge to better serve customers rather than trying to go it alone.

ABOUT THE PARTNERSHIP ECOSYSTEM

At first the idea was not popular; today it is absolutely critical to success in the industry. Enterprise-level software platforms and products need to immerse themselves within a scalable network or ecosystem of partners to grow. For example, the Salesforce ecosystem is the largest in the world. Channel sales/strategic alliances are effective because they allow you to scale at a much faster rate than through an internal direct sales team alone.

Below are a few key examples of types of partners you can form strategic alliances with:

IMPLEMENTATION CONSULTANCIES

Implementation consultancies like EY, PWC and Deloitte handle integrations, configurations, and training as part of their core businesses. Forming an alliance with large implementation consultancies like this is a great way to get in with a significant set of customers you wouldn't have access to independently.

STRATEGY CONSULTANCIES

Strategy consulting firms like McKinsey, Bain and BCG get in front of CEOs and discuss high level outcomes. They are closely aligned with our target customers and are in a position to recommend software solutions. These consultancies want to add as much value to their clients as they can and are often looking for software solutions to add to the enterprise value creations approaches they bring to their clients.

TECHNICAL ALLIANCES

Does your product have shortcomings that can be filled by a partner? What holes does your product fill for other technologies? The answers to these questions are opportunities for you to go-to-market with other technology firms. This is a mutually beneficial partnership in which you leverage your relationships and your partner leverages their relationships to achieve growth for both companies in the partnership.

DISTRIBUTION CHANNELS

You can also sell through third-parties who collect a commission on individual sales. This approach can include resellers, small independent sellers, and referral programs (e.g. 10% commission if you identify a lead, 10% if you help close it.)It is a beneficial model because it allows you to capitalize on the network of connections and foundation of trust your channel partners have already built.

KEYS TO SUCCESS:

- Build Long Term Relationships: Partnerships are the most lucrative when they are long term. That is why it is important to identify partners with aligned values, compatible sales processes, and a working knowledge of your product over time.

- Choose Complementary Partners: Choose partners that fill a gap in your offering, or you fill a gap in theirs that their customer demands. Your partners should share your target audience and have sophisticated expertise about your industry.

HOW TO FORM STRATEGIC PARTNERSHIPS:

There is no quick-and-dirty way to form strong strategic alliances. They come with time. The process often requires closing one deal, doing good work, and continually keeping in touch with the people you have relationships with. As we discussed in the authenticity chapter, much of relationship building and successful relationships is based on a gut feeling. You know when you jive with an organization;you know what moves the needle on a deal;and you start to understand more and more about who influences a deal (including both internal executives and external entities such as legal, accounting and strategy advisors). The key here is to take a long-term view and to ensure you expect to give more than you take.

- Ben Pastro, former President of Apps Associates and 25-year of the software industry.

PRIVATE EQUITY GO-TO-MARKET

So the first four models have become pretty commonplace amongst cloud software companies, but we feel we have helped create one that is more reliable, maintainable and executable than the others. That doesn't mean that the others are unimportant. They are incredibly important and absolutely paramount to most SaaS operating plans.

However, since we were personally two of the earliest SaaS movers to a Private Equity Go-To-Market selling model, we are a bit biased and remain staunchly committed to this selling approach.

The first company that heavily invested in this model is payroll, HR, and tax services company ADP in the later part of the 00's. Since then, it has been methodically levered into the SaaS ecosystem. However, many SaaS companies are missing the boat by not quickly and fully committing to this model. In simple terms, we believe this is the most efficient and effective relationship-based sales channel, bar none.

This model works based off of a private equity company's portfolio. Established private equity companies often have a large number of companies within their portfolio. When software companies align themselves with those private equity companies, they gain access to their portfolio and the operating executives at each of those companies.

Private equity (PE) companies have operating partners or/ or advisors that work with their operating companies. These individuals have exceptional executive operating experience and/ or a Big Four Partner pedigree. Only the best and brightest can excel in this demanding role. They spend their days driving new processes and business strategies that increase enterprise business value across the PE portfolio. In years past, their work focused mainly on financial re-engineering and cost cutting. Today, they are also tasked with driving growth for companies within the portfolio.

This is a strong opportunity area for sales executives today because PE fundraising is breaking records: from $60B in 2010 to a record $301B in 2019.And even with slowdowns from COVID-19, private equity fundraising remains a significant portion of US GDP.

Even with COVID-19 at full throttle, 58% of Private Equity CFO's expect to launch a new fund this year; 76% expected the new fund to be larger than the last fund they raised. [6] In total, Private Equity Assets Under Management (AUM) has surpassed $4T in 2020.

Fundraising is not only growing, but exit trends are also slowing, which means PE firms need to operate and grow companies in their portfolio now more than ever. Cloud software helps companies re-engineer finances, streamline processes to cut costs, and grow. The combination of the high-talent operating partners with the value cloud software solutions offer creates an ideal environment to sell cloud software products and services on a scale once thought impossible. When you can put your company in a position to deliver great service for one company in a portfolio, you earn introductions across the portfolio.

The model is based on one simple concept: happy customers are

6 https://assets.ey.com/content/dam/ey-sites/ey-com/en_gl/topics/private-equity/private-equity-pdfs/ey-is-your-next-step-about-changing-direction-or-directing-change.pdf

the best salespeople.

THE PROCESS

Selling in partnership with PE companies is not a traditional sales process. It cannot be forced. As we've discussed in several chapters of this book, you must be a trusted advisor with a willingness to solve problems, not a salesperson with a pre-packaged solution. That concept is critical within the PE model because it requires strategic thinking, patience, and a genuine inclination to respect and serve others.

Like everything else in cloud software, relationships, and the value you provide, is what will drive your success. If you deliver more than you promise and your solution is effective, the operations partner will introduce you to the entire portfolio. If you drop the proverbial ball or your solution does not deliver, you will be shut down across the portfolio. For good or bad, it is that simple.

Mark has so much confidence in the Private Equity Go-To-Market (GTM) that he now focuses on the approach almost exclusively. He began the strategy, right after business school, before he even knew he was doing it.. This model allows you to get in front of one operating executive that can and will, after proving your company's products or services value, introduce you to more companies across their portfolio.

CHAPTER TAKEAWAYS

BUILD LONG TERM RELATIONSHIPS:
Partnerships are the most lucrative when they are long term. That is why it is important to identify partners with aligned values, compatible sales processes, and a working knowledge of your

product over time.

CHOOSE COMPLEMENTARY PARTNERS:

Choose partners that fill a gap in your offering, or you fill a gap in theirs that their customer demands. Your partners should share your target audience and have sophisticated expertise about your industry. The alliance is mutually beneficial because it allows the PE company to standardize the value they provide across the portfolio. They can build a playbook that they pitch potential portfolio acquisitions.

CLOUD TITAN:
KLAUS BESIER, MEMBER BOARD OF DIRECTORS AT SUVODA, MAVENLINK, SEVENLAKES, AND PRAMATA

Pioneering the Strategic Alliance Ecosystem and Go-To-Market Model for Enterprise Software

ABOUT KLAUS BESIER

Klaus is a 35-year titan of enterprise software sales. Most recently, he served as Chairman and CEO of RES Software. Over the course of his career he has helped several major enterprise software solutions grow significantly. This included taking Firepond public in one of the most successful IPOs of 2000 and driving transformation of Neoware that led to an acquisition by HP. Besier is well known for his role as President and CEO of SAP America where he pioneered the channel/partnership sales approach and grew revenue from $50 million to $1 billion within 5 years.

Few enterprise software sales titans are as intimately familiar with the impact of the evolution of technology on sales as Klaus. He has seen the industry evolve from multiple vantage points. When SAP came to the U.S. from its home country of Germany, it was clear to Klaus that it would be a huge success. But not only because it was a finely tuned software product with an unwavering following throughout Europe, but because he had a plan to quickly forge an inside track with the business elite of America.

The inside track was large accounting and consulting firms. Klaus saw the need to have a strong partner and ecosystem to scale SAP. He targeted the firms with the largest consulting practices, among them were Anderson Consulting, Deloitte & Touche, and Price Waterhouse, which have become the global behemoths, Accenture, Deloitte and PwC. Klaus knew that SAP wouldn't be able to reach the Fortune 100 businesses he was targeting without partnering with an organization who already had relationships at the C level at those companies.

Klaus drove the charge to develop a strategic partner ecosystem and alliances that he believes are the reason SAP is so wildly successful today. SAP had the essentials: a strong set of products and a disciplined business process . But, instead of focusing on building a larger internal sales staff, Klaus knew he needed to align with strategic consulting firm partners.

The need for strategic partnerships became clearer than ever with SAP launched R3, an enterprise-wide information system designed to coordinate all resources, information, and activities needed to complete business processes. It was clear that SAP would be successful and there was a high demand for a force of trained and certified SAP implementation consultants. SAP had to be selective about its partners, but not exclusive.

As it turned out, they needed 5,000 consultants trained on SAP

ASAP in relatively short order, so they invited everyone from the major firms to Dallas to educate them on the opportunity. The firms that got on board early and trained the most consultants were the most successful in securing business. The other firms were forced to play catch up.

It was a win-win scenario. When SAP's partners won business, SAP won business. Since R3 was wildly popular and help was always needed to implement, the partners that had qualified resources to help win business.

Klaus also drove one of the earliest fully focused industry vertical models. It coordinated well with the way his accounting and consulting partners went to market. The large firms each had a specialty—chemicals, high tech, discrete manufacturing, consumer packaged goods, pharma, and others. SAP built competency centers for each vertical in regional hubs across the country and incentivized their partner organizations based on customer satisfaction. This combination of incentives, expertise, and regional focus allowed SAP to provide exceptional quality while scaling quickly. This immediately had an exponential impact as credibility and good work begets more and more work. The system fueled itself and SAP became the number one application software product on the planet.

SAP scaled in record time. Before competitors could catch up, SAP had a competitive advantage because they had a strong product and a robust ecosystem to help them scale fast. Ultimately, the key to a successful strategic partnership ecosystem is being "strategic" about how you select your partners, nurturing the relationships over time, and ensuring the partners you choose are aligned with your values and add value to your customers. Be open minded about partnership and enter strategic alliances that allow customers to pick the solution that is best for their company.

In the future Klaus predicts that partner and channel selling will continue to evolve and be essential for companies to thrive. There are still companies that feel that only their company can implement their product or solution. Klaus believes that that kind of us-against-them mentality will lead to obsolescence. Successful strategic partner ecosystems require that you think beyond 1-2 partners and build a large network. If you do not think across hosting platforms and technologies, you will automatically exclude your product from certain segments. The companies that prioritize partnerships will outpace and win over companies that don't put an emphasis on partnerships.

HERE ARE KLAUS'S TWO SIMPLE TIPS FOR EARNING THE TRUST, RESPECT, AND LOYALTY OF YOUR CUSTOMERS AND PARTNERS:

- Put yourself in your customer's shoes. In sales, you are nothing without empathy. Effective sales and leadership require putting yourself in your customer's shoes and taking time to understand their pain points.

- Be honest about where you can add value and where you can't. There's no reason to pull wool over anyone's eyes in sales. You will have longer term gains if you are honest and real every step of the way.

#9 | # HIRING RIGHT

USING BEHAVIORAL SCIENCE TO HIRE
AND COACH EFFECTIVELY

"There are two types of people in the world. Those who come in the room and way, 'Well, here I am!' and those who come into the room and say, 'Ah, there you are!'"

- Frederick Collins, American Scientist

Effectively leading a sales team requires perfecting a balance between exerting pressure and getting out of your team's way. Retaining a solid sales team takes an extremely refined form of leadership rooted in fairness and discipline. However, before you can effectively lead and retain an outstanding sales team, you need to carefully build your team. Building a successful sales team is one of the hardest things to accomplish in business. Throughout the course of our careers we have found that hiring the right people, taking time to understand what motivates them, consistently interacting with them individually, and operating at a strategic level is the key to succeeding as a sales leader.

Sales is a competitive space and competition is fierce for good talent, especially in the SaaS ecosystem. If you are a sales leader, you have or will experience employee poaching. There is always someone willing to recruit people out from your company. Your best defense against this is creating an environment and a culture in which people want to work. Hiring right and retaining great people has a ripple effect because great people attract more great people. Part of creating a great work environment is understanding the personal and professional motivations of your staff.

As you may expect, there are many assessments (like DISC and Meyers-Briggs), consulting firms, and even behavioral psychologists that can help with the analysis of your team, individually and as a group. However, as confident as we are that these tools and individuals can help, we believe most of the heavy lifting must come from the philosophies and practices of the chief revenue officer (CRO) and his vice presidents (VP) or manager team. They must be good teachers and have a high emotional intelligence (EQ). Being in touch with your team's personality traits allows you to strategically position your team to succeed in a sustainable way. Great sales leaders play chess, not checkers.

In fact, managers who hire based on what they see and hear during the interview process may select the wrong candidate for the sales role if they look at external characteristics alone. To truly test a person's drive, determination, passion for sales, and tenacity for working through adversity, you must take a deeper look into the internal motivation or drive of your prospective hires.

In this chapter, we outline how to determine your team's intrinsic motivators and dig into some of the types of salespeople to be aware of as you build your team. The insights in this chapter can also be applied to how you can mentor your existing team and help them work better together.

DO NOT DISCOUNT THE "RELATIONSHIP BUILDER"

CEB, Inc. was founded in the Washington, DC area in 2008. CEB (now rebranded to Challenger) provides insights and technology to business leaders in a variety of fields, including sales. Two of their leaders, Mathew Dixon and Brent Adamson, published a game-changing sales book, The Challenger Sale, based on the incredible data to which they had access. The book was a vanguard piece of work because it leveraged data to back up their sales recommendations in a new, innovative way.

As Challenger has grown over the last eleven years, they have become one of the best sources of deep sales performance data and analysis in the business. They are incredible at what they do. In 2018, they were spun-off (and rebranded to "Challenger") from their structure within the Gartner Group ownership and into a PE-backed deal with Marlin Equity Partners, one of the best in the business of private equity.

However, as with any great research, there can be flaws in interpretation. Experts both internal and external to Challenger have interpreted their powerful trove of data in different ways.

First, let's start with their classifications of sales profiles. Challenger has done a fine job with their five profiles and an even better job conducting the research to attempt to determine which type or types are the most productive. As you will see later in this chapter, we have offered some additional ways to classify the behavioral characteristics of selling professionals through DISC and Meyers-Briggs methodologies and behavioral science.[6]

The problems occur when you try to put talents into a box. As we all know, everyone is different and there is no unequivocal "lone wolf" or "hard worker." There are infinite variations of the profiles Challenger has developed and the profiles we offer later in this chapter.

One disappointing part of this particular interpretation of the Challenger data is the disparagement of Relationship Selling.

6. Bryan, Jordan. "The Power of the Challenger Sales Model." Smarter With Gartner, 2019, www.gartner.com/smarterwithgartner/power-challenger-sales-model/.

THE FIVE PROFILES OF SALES PROFESSIONALS[6]

HARD WORKER
- Always goes the extra mile
- Doesn't give up easily
- Self-Motivated
- Interested in feedback and development

CHALLENGER
- Always has a different view of the world
- Understands the customer's business
- Loves to debate
- Pushes the customer

RELATIONSHIP BUILDER
- Builds strong customer advocates
- Generous in giving time to help others
- Gets along with everyone

LONE WOLF
- Follows own instincts
- Self-Assured
- Independent

PROBLEM SOLVER
- Reliably responds
- Ensures that all problems are solved
- Detail oriented

The data below suggests that Relationship-Based Sellers are not the highest performers in most sales teams. We agree, if you only focused on relationship-based methodologies and approaches you probably would struggle. However, humans and hard-driving business executives love to celebrate big wins opposed to smaller, more sustainable wins from relationships.

DO THESE MESSAGES SOUND FAMILIAR?
"We need net-new logos, go bag an elephant."

"Oh, that deal was only an add-on to an existing one or just a renewal."

"We need to sell $200M in new business to counter the churn in the business."

WHY NOT SHIFT THE PERSPECTIVE?

"There are a lot more mice and fat squirrels out there than elephants, so keep bringing them in."

"Wow, how great is it that we keep expanding that relationship year after year?"

"We only need to reduce churn by 2% and sell $100M in new logos this year to make Wall Street very happy."

So, to all of you soft-selling, friend-building, trust-based sellers out there, we salute you. Yes, we need to challenge, ask the hard questions, work extremely hard, be reliable, authentic, and creative too. However, just ask any of the top rain-making partners at the Big Four, strategy consulting, or global law firms how easy it is to find their next deal from their Salesforce rolodex. If you ask and listen, you won't ever discount the impact of relationships and a powerful network, whether it is filled with CEOs or PE operating partners or friends that you hung around with four years ago at parties on your college campus or in business school.

In fact, Challenger with Gartner's help has demonstrated in its research that relationship-focused representatives (reps) are in fact the most reliable. As we explored earlier, reliability is the bedrock to sales leadership. Your reliable reps get you past your revenue targets in good times and bad, whether luck was on your side that year or not.

PERCENTAGE OF CORE VERSUS
HIGH PERFORMERS PER PROFILE[6]

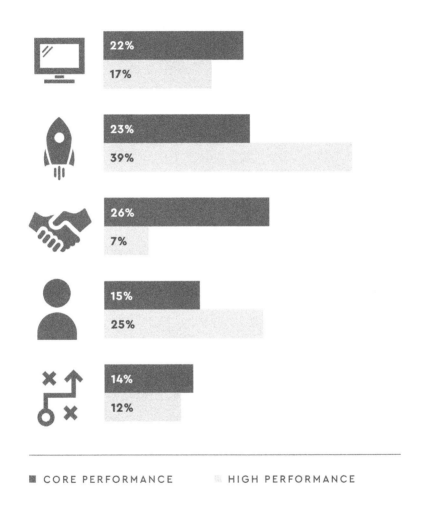

22%
17%

23%
39%

26%
7%

15%
25%

14%
12%

■ CORE PERFORMANCE   HIGH PERFORMANCE

6. Bryan, Jordan. "The Power of the Challenger Sales Model." Smarter With Gartner, 2019, www.gartner.com/smarterwithgartner/power-challenger-sales-model/.

INTRINSIC MOTIVATIONS

In 2014, and revalidated in 2020, Target Training International (TTI) published groundbreaking research that linked one of six intrinsic motivators as most important to the top salespeople in both the U.S. and Europe. They established it is the motivation/ internal drive to achieve results that is most impactful. They also discovered, "it is what's on the inside, not on the outside, that counts, especially in sales performance."

These are the "find a way" people who are extremely resourceful. You can rely on them to meet or exceed their sales targets or die trying. They see personal and corporate opportunity with multipliers built into most every SaaS compensation plan. They capture the opportunity to overperform when their territory is ripe.

SOME IDEAS FOR INTERVIEW QUESTIONS TO DETERMINE INTERNAL MOTIVATION

How do you really learn about the candidate you are interviewing? Here are a few question suggestions that we always make sure to use:

WHAT IS YOUR PASSION?

The answer shouldn't be selling. If they answer with a bunch of nonsense that their goal in life is to be an incredible sales rep, they may not be the right hire. Being a successful sales rep is a great means to many ends, but it is not an end.

DO YOU REMEMBER YOUR FIRST SALE? WHAT WAS YOUR EXPERIENCE?

Regardless of what the experience was, if you are looking for a passionate, intrinsically motivated sales rep, look for a passionate response to these questions.

WHAT WOULD YOU SAY ARE THE GRAY AREAS OF SELLING?

This broad question will showcase your interviewees ethics and creativity.

TELL ME ABOUT THE LAST THREE SALES LOSSES YOU HAD?

When you ask about losses, you will learn about your interviewee's process, determination, and character. Look for signs that they have learned from each loss and applied it to improve in other subsequent deals.

TELL ME ABOUT ADVERSITY THAT YOU HAVE HAD IN YOUR PERSONAL OR PROFESSIONAL LIFE AND HOW YOU OVERCAME IT

Your interviewee will likely share deep behavioral and mindset information as an answer to this question. This question may prompt them to talk about something personal rather than a professional loss, which will showcase how they handle adversity in life and at work and whether they are willing to share their authentic self, not a highly edited version of it.

WALK ME THROUGH THE STRUCTURE OF A DREAM COMPENSATION PLAN. HOW WOULD YOU GUIDE ME TO BUILD THE NEXT YEARLY SALES COMP PLAN?

This question will show you what motivates and drives your interviewee. Are they a risk taker? How important is money? How important is cash flow to their lifestyle? Are they willing to work as hard as necessary for the role they are being considered for?

WHAT IS MOST IMPORTANT TO YOU IN LIFE?

This opens the treasure chest. Again, it will let you know how your prospect thinks and what motivates and drives them.

SALES PROFESSIONAL STYLES

Assuming your candidates have this internal drive, you can now turn your attention to a person's sales style. Over the years, we have used the DISC Assessment personality classifications of D - Dominant, I - Influence, S – Steadiness, and C - Compliant to help us determine our team member's styles. We find that better understanding our teams helps us equip them with the tools they need to improve performance and evolve over time. These are the common styles we've encountered.

DISC WHEEL: SALES STYLES

FAUX SUPERSTAR

Our experience is that over a quarter of the company's superstars are just beneficiaries of being in the right place at the right time, and, most importantly, the right accounts. As a D, they are fast-moving drivers who are outwardly competitive and want to achieve results quickly. Their major downfall is over confidence and thinking their processes are strong since they have worked in the past. The takeaway here is to never rely solely on revenue performance as the baseline for evaluating a team member.

THE TECHNICIAN

This is the sales rep that has read all the sales books and attended every sales training session they can attend. A process-driven champion of details, they have strong process and follow up skills. On the DISC assessment, this individual usually scores a high C, high S, and reasonably high D. The technician usually does not have strong creative skills. Makes for a reliable rep in the right environment.

THE NATURAL

The Natural has an innate ability to connect with and influence others. Their weak point is that they do not build out basic process skills or push beyond the limits of their natural abilities to become a top performer. With mentoring, The Natural can become The Superstar. The Natural is usually a combination of a high D and I on the DISC assessment.

THE SUPERSTAR

The Superstar is highly intelligent, driven, process-oriented, and naturally able to connect with and influence others. They are usually very coachable, efficient, and have a high EQ. On the DISC assessment they score high on I. They are typically the most intelligent of the high I's people.

MS. OR MR. RELIABLE

These are the real professionals in our business. We will take a team mostly built from "reliables" any day of the week. They have the right mix of people skills (I) combined with extremely productive sales processes and systems (S). Externally, they manage stress very well, have a balanced approach to doing business, and just seem happier than most. Flashy Superstars and Faux Superstars may temporarily steal the spotlight, but Ms. Reliables win over the long haul. Ms. Reliables are wonderful at seeing and seizing opportunities.

THE PROFESSOR

The Professor has many of the same behavioral attributes of The Technician but are not usually the stronger sales performer. The Professor is a champion of the idea of process but is more of a theoretical thinker and less prone to acting. They are used to finding holes in any proposal and may irritate faster-moving styles. These individuals do have the foundation to become a Reliable, with proper mentoring.

THE EXPERT

These are the folks who are extremely brilliant, and they know it. They have the natural ability to see things from both a macro and micro view. In doing so, sometimes they can rub people the wrong way internally and externally. With clients who appreciate their styles, they can be your greatest sales asset. With clients who don't, they can be your biggest nightmare.

THE POWER OF TEAM SELLING

Each of the personality/sales types outlined above can be leveraged to work together. Especially in consultative sales, all personal behavior styles and motivations can be leveraged in team selling.

The natural "door openers" are the Faux Superstar, the Natural, the Superstar, and Ms. Reliable. Their styles naturally attract them to people, especially to others who are like them. Once the door is opened, the Planner is needed to structure and manage the engagement. The Technician understands the nuances of the software and can answer the clients detailed questions about the application. The Professor can address client's requests for customization capabilities. The Expert can be brought in when challenges arise by bridging the macro/micro views of the situation and how to remediate it.

Paul and I together are a perfect example of leveraging styles and motivation to lead consultative sales efforts. From a style perspective we are both squarely in "The Natural" sector. We realize the need to bring in colleagues with other strengths when intricate software customizations or system challenges arise. All the while, we maintain client relationships and act as the conduit between the client's decision makers and their technical staff. We are also alike in our ability to objectively function in any client's culture and to live on the leading edge of innovation—two unspoken characteristics that most depend on in cloud computing. We work well as a team because we support each other while driving client engagements to successful conclusions.

INTEGRATING BEHAVIORAL STYLES INTO YOUR LEADERSHIP PLAN

Whether you are a CRO or a front-line sales rep, your career will benefit from understanding what drives your colleagues. Once you understand what drives the people you interact with, you will be more effective and productive together.

For example, Paul is results driven. It is most important to him that a deal delivers a return on investment for all involved. On the other hand, Mark is most driven by a strong desire to focus on the long-term relationship above and beyond the immediate results. Our goals and incentives are most effective and motivating when they are built around what drives us. Neither approach is right or wrong independently, but can be exponentially powerful when complementary behavioral styles come together.

This same thought process can and should be utilized with your clients, prospects, and alliance partners as well. The more adept you are at understanding how people like to work and communicate, the more powerful these tools become for you.

Furthermore, it is not hard to see which DISC quadrants most individuals fall into before any assessment is taken. You can deduce someone's personality type through knowing their title and role, interaction style, meeting style, how much personal info they share, and how many questions they ask you about yourself. For example, there are not too many CFOs out there that are not high Cs (Compliance); however, that can change based on company needs. We have seen CFOs that have been hired with a very high baseline I (Influence) brought in to lead significant business process change or to champion other initiatives that aren't completely focused on the numbers or regulatory requirements of the business.

Another example is when you walk into an executive office and you notice that they are relatively curt about engaging in pleasantries. When you ask them about the picture of their family vacation in Fiji and they answer, "It was a nice trip," you should take the hint and adjust your meeting style. In other words, get straight to business, stick to key facts and the quantitative impact of your product, and finish on time. Lower I and high C and S individuals appreciate your ability to stay organized, on task, and respectful of their time. If they interrupt you to get the meeting started, they are likely a high D as well.

Though there are trends, there is no one personality combination that automatically equates to a top performing sales representative. Top performers can have quite different behavioral characteristics and personality traits. The trick is finding out the combination of individual motivators and drivers that are right for your team and to make sure you integrate that information into your management, coaching, and motivation.

Look at a person's motivation first and personal style second. Anyone who knows themselves and what they uniquely bring to the table can be an asset in the sales continuum. Integrating and leveraging behavioral styles into your leadership plan requires a combination of gut instinct and science. When done right, the result will be an effective and productive "go-to-market" team.

DIVERSITY IN SALES

When it is time to establish a relationship or make a sale, customers and prospects are not one single race, gender, or ethnicity. Yet, in the sales profession, the workforce does not reflect the melting pot diversity in this country. As stated in the "Women in Sales" callout section in Chapter 3, though women make up 50% of the population, they represent only 39% of the sales industry, and just 19% are in leadership positions. This underrepresentation trend is similar when it comes to race. Recent data from the U.S. Census Bureau reports that in the sales industry, 78.3% of workers are White, 5.8% African American, 7.7% Asian, and 6.9% Hispanic/Latino. However, 14% of the U.S. population are African Americans, and of the 5.8% in the sales industry only 3.2% of those are in senior leadership roles at large companies. Although these numbers have slightly improved over time in favor of diversity, there is tremendous room for growth and improvement.

Although there is currently a lack of diversity in the industry, diversity in your sales team is beneficial in multiple ways; it boosts performance, fosters team innovation, and is linked to increased sales and profits. Here are just a few reasons you should prioritize diversity on your sales team:

A DIVERSE TEAM HELPS YOU BUILD MORE MEANINGFUL CONNECTIONS WITH PROSPECTS

Intentional or not, salespeople often naturally appeal to those who look and/or have backgrounds similar to themselves, which isolates potential prospects. If a prospect has a different background than you, and you have no experience with diversity, it is going to be nearly impossible to connect with them and build trust.

The Harvard Business Review conducted a study that found that a team with a member who shares a client's ethnicity is 152% more likely to understand that client than another team.[8] Therefore, it stands to reason that increasing the diversity of your sales team will help you better serve potential prospects. A diverse team of sales reps will form stronger customer relationships, be more profitable, and stay with their companies longer. Cedric Herring, a member of the University of Illinois at Chicago sociology department and professor of sociology and public policy at the University of Illinois' Institute of Government and Public Affairs, found that diversity has a positive effect on financial revenue. His research discovered companies who reported the highest levels of racial diversity

7. Sylvia Ann Hewlett, Melinda Marshall and Laura Sherbin. "How Diversity Can Drive Innovation." Harvard Business Review, 1 Aug. 2014, hbr.org/2013/12/how-diversity-can-drive-innovation.

brought in, on average, nearly 15 times more sales revenue than companies who reported the lowest levels of racial diversity.

"A non-diverse environment doesn't foster innovation, it's not flexible, it just produces more of the same ideas. Lack of innovation and creativity is the death of any company today— the markets are changing too fast to allow survival of companies that sit still."

-Gabe Larson, VP of Growth at InsideSales.com

YOUR TEAM WANTS TO WORK IN AN INCLUSIVE ENVIRONMENT

A SalesLoft survey found a near-unanimous desire, among consumers and sales professionals for a workforce with an inclusive environment that is more representative and diverse overall. Specifically, 91% of consumers and sales professionals want to see increased racial diversity. The problem is often that companies do not know where to start or how to increase diversity. However, as Tash Jefferies, Co-Founder of Hirekind says, "People of under-represented groups don't expect perfection in efforts."[8] If you are not sure where to start or need help, search for organizations outside of your company that can help with hiring diversity and inclusion or provide assistance and education to the company.

REMEMBER: DIVERSITY DOES NOT EQUAL INCLUSION

Diversity does not automatically equal inclusion. Hiring a diverse workforce does not mean the environment they are hired into is inviting. Some companies and work environments are rife with unconscious biases and stereotypes that then manifest themselves into microaggressions. These elements make a toxic work environment preventing inclusion and diversity of any kind. These can prevent people of color from applying to a company or force the talented people of color who already work there to leave. Sometimes it is hard to recognize the destructive effects of unconscious biases, stereotypes, and microaggressions, but that does not mean they do not exist. Here are a few tips for making a more inclusive environment:

1. Educate employees on unconscious bias and commit to mitigating bias when speaking to colleagues and prospects. This could mean hiring an outside firm or resource to train employees on unconscious bias and microaggressions. Provide resources for employees to learn more about the negative effects of stereotypes and microaggressions.

2. Nurture a culture of openness so if employees are having problems with microaggressions, racism, or any toxic issue they feel comfortable approaching you. Additionally, encourage employees to reflect on their own actions for improvement.

3. Lead the way and surround yourself with individuals who can help you identify biases. Be willing to listen and learn. Observe your own behavior and self-reflect on your actions.

4. Take diversity and inclusion seriously. Be an ally and someone who can advocate for why biases, stereotypes, and microaggressions are harmful.

"A diverse workforce that thrives in an inclusive culture leads to a better ability to serve customers, a higher level of innovation, and a stronger employer brand."

– Art Hopkins, consultant at Russell Reynolds Associates

---

8. Kidane, Merhawi. "Why Increasing Your Sales Team Diversity Improves Your Bottom Line." Nutshell, 20 Dec. 2019, www.nutshell.com/blog/increasing-sales-team-diversity/.

In an inspirational sense, humans want to see someone similar to themselves/who looks like them in high-level positions so they can say "I can do it because so-and-so did." Otherwise, some individuals do not consider that career or life path. By increasing diversity in the sales workforce now and working to promote or hire diverse talent in leadership positions, the industry is guaranteeing an increase of diversity in the future. And, by maintaining unconscious bias and microaggression training, the sales industry is creating and maintaining a work environment of awareness and promoting inclusion and understanding.

CHAPTER TAKEAWAYS

BUILDING A SUCCESSFUL SALES TEAM IS ONE OF THE HARDEST THINGS TO ACCOMPLISH IN BUSINESS, HERE'S WHAT TO PRIORITIZE:

- Focus on hiring culture fits.
- Take time to understand what motivates your team members.
- Consistently take time to interact individually with your team.

CULTURE WINS

- There is always someone willing to recruit people out of a company. Your best defense against this is creating an environment and a culture in which people want to work.

INVEST IN GETTING TO KNOW WHAT MOTIVATES YOUR TEAM

- Part of creating a great work environment is understanding the personal and professional motivations of your staff.
- Being in touch with your team's personality traits allows you to strategically position your team to succeed in a sustainable way. Great sales leaders play chess, not checkers.

CLOUD TITAN:
MYRON RADIO, PRESIDENT,
THE R GROUP, LLC

The Power of Matching Style and Motivation when Hiring and Managing Sales Professionals

ABOUT MYRON

Five-time author and President/Founder of The R Group, LLC (TRG), a consortium of seasoned professionals who specialize in the human dynamics of executive and organizational Change & Strategy Execution, Myron Radio is recognized as a world-renowned professional behavioral analyst (CPBA Certified), speaker, team builder, and executive coach.

A small government company had a somewhat unique product and service that would aid the war fighter in combat. After ten years in the business, they were positioning themselves for explosive growth. They needed a seasoned, well-connected business development (BD) leader to spearhead the effort.

Working through a retained search firm, they found what they thought to be the perfect candidate. Johnny had both small and large government contractor experience. He had worked on several committees with the key client decision makers. He even lived close to the main client's office, reducing the commute time between the firms.

In the interview, Johnny appeared knowledgeable, professional, and personable. Everyone who met him thought he was a perfect fit for the job. As a result, he was selected and quickly began to build the BD organization for the future.

Five months later, Myron Radio got a call to be Johnny's coach. Since he started, Johnny had been focused on building the BD infrastructure and reporting applications that would accommodate the company's growth. While there were plenty of client and staff meetings, no new prospects or contracts entered their sales pipeline.

As part of Radio's coaching engagement, Johnny completed a multi-lens personal assessment. It included a DISC behavior style, motivation, and personal skills/competency segments. At the same time, he conducted an interview-based 360 assessment on Johnny's interactions with others. Finally, he developed a Role Profile with the principles at the firm to get a clear view of (1) what they expected of a BD leader, (2) how performance would be measured, and (3) the "ideal" combination of the person's style, motivation, and competencies that would lead to success.

When comparing Johnny's personal data to the Role Profile, Radio found him to be a total mismatch on all styles and motivation criteria. In other words, Johnny had the exact opposite of what the company needed in a BD leader to achieve success.

Johnny was moved to a consultant status to leverage his strong network, infrastructure know-how, and professional network. The company used the Role Profile to attract, select, and deploy a new BD leader who hit the ground running to fill the pipeline with proposals and new market opportunities.

TITAN TIPS

- A traditional job description alone is not enough to select the right candidate for your key position. To hire well, you need to be crystal clear on key areas of focus, performance goals, measures of success, and the personal style, motivation, and competencies of the ideal (to the best of your knowledge) candidate for the role.

- A behavioral assessment alone is not enough to predict success. While valuable in and of itself, too many false assumptions can be made based on a single lens view. When filling critical roles, due diligence regarding knowledge, experience, relationships, networks, culture-fit, style, motivation, and competencies are required.

- Surround yourself with people who compliment your skill set and make you better. Build a team with your recipe of the right level of connectedness and diverseness with a focus on productivity building, team energy-creation, and blind-spot coverage.

#10 | CUSTOMER SUCCESS

GROWTH THROUGH SUPPORT AND SERVICE
OF YOUR CURRENT CUSTOMERS

"It's amazing to consider that no matter what size customer we were pitching, or where in the world we were selling, a singular idea drove all our accomplishments: we never sold features. We sold the model and we sold the customer's success."

- Marc Benioff, Behind the Cloud: The Untold Story of How salesforce.com Went from Idea to Billion-Dollar Company-and Revolutionized an Industry

Customer Success as a business discipline began in the early 2000s due to the shift from contract-based software sales to the SaaS pricing model. This shift has demanded much higher engagement between software vendors and customers. Contracts used to be huge deals with smaller maintenance fees. Today, in the SaaS model, customers pay a monthly or quarterly fee and can much more easily disengage from a software vendor than ever before.

Since our customers have more options than ever before, if we do not deliver a positive customer experience, we will lose customers. It is a hugely important function because customer success is responsible for earning additional recurring revenue from existing customers. They work to improve customer retention (also referred to as reduced churn), grow revenue, and improve customer satisfaction and experience.

It is so easy to get caught up in thinking that new accounts are more special than established accounts. That type of machismo thinking is outdated and counterproductive. Paul and I will take increased installed base revenue all day long and have always invested very heavily in talented farmers. Just like any good soccer or field hockey team, you don't just need star forwards who can score, you need strong defense too. It is no different in a world-class cloud software sales organization.

WHAT IS CUSTOMER SUCCESS?

It is a methodology that focuses on ensuring customers achieve their goals while using your product or service. Many companies have roles solely dedicated to customer success: Customer Success Managers (CSMs). CSMs focus their time on building relationships with existing clients. Their goal is to align client objectives with the growth of the software company. This role is valuable for two reasons: first, it increases up-sell opportunities, second and more importantly, it reduces customer turnover. It is much less expensive to keep a client than to bring on a new one. Overall, customer success improves customer lifetime value for the company and can immensely improve a customer experience.

SELL LIKE TODD BEAMER

Todd Beamer is the hero who, with a few other very special passengers, saved many lives on September 11, 2001 by fighting the terrorists on United Flight 93 and stopping them from crashing into our Capital Building. He is known for the words "Let's Roll" that have become synonymous with our country's fight against terror. He was also a friend and business associate of Mark's.

Mark heard him say "Let's Roll" more than once on the way to grabbing a quick sandwich between meetings or running out to a client call together when they worked together at Oracle Corporation. Todd was an exceptionally successful sales representative and manager, but more importantly he was a loving husband, a committed father, a man of immense character, and integrity.

The first Customer Success leader Mark ever worked day-to-day with was Todd Beamer. Todd had never held an official "customer success" title. However, he built some of the tenets of the discipline of Customer Success without ever knowing what he built. He was a sales representative and sales manager, but he sold very differently from most of the other sales reps at Oracle. He always exceeded his quotas while delivering a host of additional support services that very much resemble what customer success teams deliver today.

What he delivered to his clients was a full-service approach that was, even then, completely focused on making his customers successful. He dove deeply into the business model of his respective clients, did the required research, and asked all the right questions. He compiled best practices across his client base and appropriately shared ideas based on the most successful process flows. This insight he gained from all these efforts allowed Todd to be a more effective advocate for his clients within Oracle and in turn they often recommended Todd to other companies and brought more business to Todd every quarter.

ABOUT THE CUSTOMER SUCCESS MANAGER ROLE

CSMs are the main point of contact on client accounts. They cover the responsibilities of traditional account managers/ project managers/ technical account managers, but their responsibilities are primarily focused on generating long-term value to customers. Essentially, they want to maximize the amount of value the customer generates from using their solution. They are responsible for relentlessly monitoring and managing how the customer uses the solution. They deeply understand what motivates the customer and continually strive to provide more value and to help the customer get the most out of their solution. This often includes:

TECHNICAL ENABLEMENT
CSMs help users set up the solution, supporting all training and onboarding needs.

KNOWLEDGE ENABLEMENT
CSMs make sure customers are well-informed about the solution and newest functions. This can include newsletters, check-in phone calls, webinars, events, and customer portal communication.

OPPORTUNITY AND RISK ASSESSMENT
CSMs are responsible for reviewing each account periodically, understanding the primary reasons the customer uses the tool, and asking how the tool could better help the client achieve their goals. Part of the role is also assessing how likely the client is to leave and intervening when issues arise.

ACCOUNT MANAGEMENT
The CSM role goes far beyond traditional account management, but it does include some of those traditional responsibilities: ensuring contract renewal, upselling, and working as an advocate for the customer to various groups in the organization.

WHAT DOES IT TAKE TO SUCCEED IN CUSTOMER SUCCESS?

Bain Research interviewed 70 customer success leaders at top tech companies about the most important aspects of their jobs and their performance in those areas. The top performers reported the keys to their success as a positive attitude, ability to work well with others, tendency to be big-picture thinkers, and ability to help customers help themselves.

WHAT SEPARATES CUSTOMER SUCCESS LEADERS IN TECH?[9]

How technology vendors can make sure their customers are capturing the most value from their products and services

---

TECH FIRMS HAVE WORK TO DO ON CUSTOMER SUCCESS

Bain surveyed 70 customer success leaders at tech companies and found that...

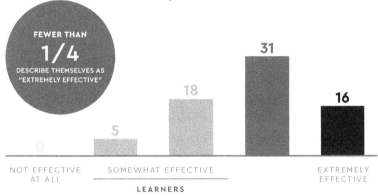

FEWER THAN 1/4 DESCRIBE THEMSELVES AS "EXTREMELY EFFECTIVE"

| 0 | 5 | 18 | 31 | 16 |

NOT EFFECTIVE AT ALL · SOMEWHAT EFFECTIVE · EXTREMELY EFFECTIVE

LEARNERS

LEADERS MAKE BETTER USE OF THEIR TIME

When compared to customer success learners, leaders spent:

BUILDING CUSTOMER RELATIONSHIPS

PROACTIVELY CHECKING IN

MONITORING ADOPTION

36% MORE TIME

47% LESS TIME

DEALING WITH SUPPORT ISSUES AND ESCALATIONS

Since the sales team is primarily responsible for driving that level of growth, having a reliable process is crucial. If you are part of a young and rapidly growing company, exceeding 40% growth should not be much of a challenge. The true challenge lies in keeping up that level of growth as an older company. One effective strategy to keep profit margins growing is to tap into the growth potential of your current customers. As you can see in the chart below, maintaining the rule of 40 year over year is difficult.

CONSISTENTLY OUTPERFORMING THE RULE OF 40 IS DIFFICULT[9]

Out of 53 companies that outperformed the Rule of 40,
22 did so for three or more years

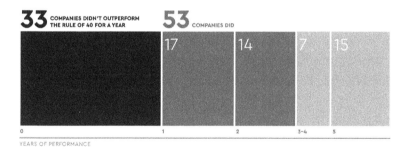

"*As growth slows, mature software companies look for ways to generate more revenue from existing customers, while becoming more efficient to increase profit margins and maintain performance that beats the Rule of 40.*"

- Hacking Software's Rule of 40, Bain

Ted Malley, former global leader of Customer Success for both Ceridian and Ultimate Software has earned his notable career success by understanding how to maximize the gold within his company's existing customer portfolio. His best advice? Make your customers the heroes of your company story. Without this level of customer advocacy it becomes extremely difficult to sustain the rule of 40, even for the most productive selling organizations. The competitive advantage of a loyal and enthusiastic customer base due to a powerful Customer Success function is absolutely imperative to sustained growth.

Large companies such as Salesforce and Adobe have achieved the Rule of 40 by developing new products and markets adjacent to their core and have navigated well business model transitions such as the move to SaaS and subscription models. This type of evolution is key.

"Customers are the biggest asset of a mature software business. Retaining that base, and expanding the value delivered to it, becomes the top priority. Ensuring customer success, investing in customer-centric innovation, developing broader and deeper solutions strategies, and implementing pricing strategies and discipline are all essential." Hacking Software's Rule of 40, Bain

So, what customer data does your company have that can help you learn more about the best way to serve your customers and move to a "farming" vs. "hunting" approach? How could you establish more efficient ways of selling to establish customers? These are the questions that successful sales organizations are asking, answering, and acting on.

9. "Infographic: What Separates Customer Success Leaders in Tech?" Bain, 1 Apr. 2020, www.bain.com/insights/customer-success-tech-infographic/.

CHAPTER TAKEAWAYS

Customer Success as a business discipline began in the early 2000s due to the shift from contract-based software sales to the SaaS pricing model.

- This shift has demanded much higher engagement between software vendors and customers.

- Contracts used to be huge deals with smaller maintenance fees. Today, in the SaaS model, customers pay a monthly or quarterly fee and can much more easily disengage from a software vendor than ever before.

Since our customers have more options than ever before, if we do not deliver a positive customer experience, we will lose customers.

- Customer success professionals serve a hugely important role because customer success is responsible for earning additional recurring revenue from existing customers and to improve client retention.

Believing that new accounts are more special than established accounts is outdated and counterproductive.

- Paul and we will take increased installed base revenue all day long and have always invested very heavily in talented farmers.

- Just like any good soccer or field hockey team, you don't just need star forwards who can score, you need strong defense too. It is no different in a world-class cloud software sales organization.

MARC BENIOFF, MARIA MARTINEZ: CUSTOMER SUCCESS CHAMPIONS

Mark worked with Oracle for 20 years as a partner and as an employee. During this time, he had the opportunity to work with some of the most amazing enterprise software minds in the business. Paul had the same opportunity during his time at SAP. One of the most exceptional software sales minds Mark encountered was Marc Benioff: Founder and CEO of Salesforce.

Mark's first clue that Benioff was assuredly confident in launching Salesforce was the fact that Benioff was leaving a very lucrative Senior Vice President (SVP) position at Oracle to do so. When Benioff launched Salesforce in March 1999, a key component of his strategy was delivering a level of customer partnership and experience that was very different from what the major player, Oracle, SAP, and Microsoft, were offering at the time. He defined Salesforce's mission as "The End of Software." By that he meant the end of software as we knew it and a major transition to what we now know as Software as a Service (SaaS).

The cloud titan featured in the next section, Maria Martinez, served as Salesforce's first Global Leader of Customer Success (and current Chief Customer Experience Officer at Cisco). She built a team of over 4,000 professionals entirely focused on helping customers succeed in achieving their business goals with the help of Salesforce's exceptional product suite.

Martinez had done this before. She was one of the first to drive an effective customer success model throughout a large, global company starting all the way back in 2003 at Microsoft. She was one of the best before joining up with Benioff. However, the duo took the art of customer success to a new level. They unleashed billions of dollars of additional enterprise value at Salesforce by supporting hundreds of thousands of Salesforce customers every day, in an entirely new way. Even though he has never held the title, Marc Benioff, has been the most effective customer success leader to date. But he never would have been able to build the dynasty he built without the support of incredible customer success leaders like Maria.

TIP:

To get an additional leg up in customer success, we suggest reading Nick Mehta, CEO of Gainsight's enlightening book *Customer Success*. The book outlines how to reduce churn and grow revenue faster than your competitors.

CLOUD TITAN:
MARIA MARTINEZ, CISCO, EXECUTIVE VICE PRESIDENT AND CHIEF CUSTOMER EXPERIENCE OFFICER; BOARD DIRECTOR AT MCKESSON AND THE SILICON VALLEY EDUCATION FOUNDATION

Tips from a Leading Innovator in SaaS Customer Success and Customer Experience

ABOUT MARIA

As a member of the executive leadership team, Martinez oversees Cisco's $13B Services and Customer Success organizations. At her core, Maria, is a hardware engineer. She started her career building switches, and only transitioned to customer-facing roles when she joined Microsoft to lead sales for its telecommunications and media sectors. This shift eventually led to her position driving Customer Success at Salesforce, and now, Customer Experience (CX) at Cisco. What's the difference, you may ask, between customer success and customer experience?

According to Martinez, customer experience is the end-to-end customer journey, and Customer Success is a component of customer experience.

Customer Experience begins at the point of need for the customer. It addresses these key questions:

- What is the problem the customer is trying to solve?

- What is the customer's goal?

- What products or practices do we have that can help them achieve their goals and solve the problems they need to solve?

Customer Success begins post-sale, and it addresses these key questions:

- How is the customer able to adopt and use the product?

- How well is the customer achieving value through the product?

Martinez was a trailblazer in strategizing around these questions at Salesforce, particularly in bridging the gap between the sale of a product or service and its renewal. She built processes and systems that fortify a customer's positive experience by automating and simplifying customer follow-up and support.

Today, at Cisco, Martinez and her team are innovating to simplify customer experience. The core philosophy driving their innovation is that a company's value does not lie solely in its product, but rather, in how it engages and supports its customers. So, while Cisco's products and services are complex in their capabilities, Martinez and her team are working hard to ensure they are intuitive and simple for Cisco customers. According to Martinez, simplicity is one of the hardest things to achieve, it requires an optimal balance of engineering, marketing, and sales, synergizing to forge a seamless path for customers to solve their problems, achieve their goals, and achieve more and more value through use of the product.

TITAN TIPS:

1. Be customer obsessed. Have a deep knowledge of your customer, it is the best way to accelerate their success.

2. Earn trust by proactively anticipating customer needs. Know customer needs and quickly act to address their challenges.

3. Simplify. Use the customer experience as a simplification agent and unifier of customer-facing efforts across the company.

4. Develop a comprehensive customer journey. Every interaction is an opportunity to add value and create a differentiated experience for the customer.

5. Always be innovating! Differentiated customer experiences are often the best competitive advantage a company has.

TECHNOLOGIES: SALES STACK

#11

ARTIFICIAL INTELLIGENCE IS SUPERCHARGING THE WAY WE SELL. LEVERAGE IT INTELLIGENTLY.

"Technology is a useful servant but a dangerous master."

- Christian Lous Lange, Historian, Teacher, and Political Scientist

We have talked a lot in this book about the importance of humanity in the future of sales. Trust. Empathy. Creativity. Authenticity. Passion. These are all deeply human traits. It's true that most sales decisions are emotional. However, sales planning and execution is increasingly augmented by technology. We will not ignore the importance of human beings in sales, but we would be remiss if we ignore the artificial intelligence and technology currently revolutionizing the way we sell.

Artificial intelligence (AI) is defined by the Oxford dictionary as "the theory and development of computer systems able to perform tasks that normally require human intelligence, such as visual perception, speech recognition, decision-making, and translation between languages" However, it is important not to think of AI as our replacement. Instead, think of it as a tool to enhance the way you work. As we mentioned earlier in the book, those of us who have chosen sales as a career are much better protected than many other career choices. Robots are coming, but a robot version of the selling genius, Tommy from the movie "Tommy Boy" is likely not going to be produced anytime soon.

*"Successful sales efforts today hinge on digital tools—
maintaining a robust digital infrastructure, deploying the right
applications and mining digital data to bring insights to the
field are all crucial ingredients."*

- Bain

Whether you are new to sales or a veteran, technology can save you time and help guide your sales strategy. Tools like Salesforce, Outreach.io, People.ai, SalesLoft, Gainsight, and Microsoft Dynamics show us insights and eliminate mundane legwork.

In the past, we had to learn the hard way that we were spending too much time on the wrong deals. We combed through notes to determine which sales approaches were working and which were falling flat. Today, technology can help us arrive at these conclusions sooner, remind us when to change course, and suggest tailored approaches for each prospect.

As Shannon Copeland, Chief Operating Officer of N3, shared in the April edition of Selling Power magazine, "We can simply move faster than our competitors." Shannon continued, "It's all about exceptional culture, people, and processes, combined with the right tech." And, while corporate giants and N3 customers such as Microsoft, Cisco, IBM, and SAP may have layers of tech supporting marketing and sales, N3 strives to synthesize signals and make the tech invisible to the agents. "As a BPO, efficiency, results,and low costs are our trade secrets, our craft," Copeland says, "We deliver the relative disruptive growth our clients demand at maximum efficiency and in a style and manner that improves our clients' brands among their current and future customers."As Shannon points out, the sky's the limit when you have powerful technology, well-designed processes, and talented people.

Think of your CRM and any other tech tools you use as a combination of a mentor and administrative assistant. In other words, let technology handle the more routine, repetitive tasks and give insight to inform your go-to-market and prospecting plans. Doing so will liberate your time and allow you to invest your energy in better deals. When you spend less time creating reports and pouring over notes, you spend more time out in the world selling and building real relationships.

EMBRACE ARTIFICIAL INTELLIGENCE, IT IS HERE TO STAY

"AI is probably the most important thing humanity has ever worked on."

- Sundar Pichai, CEO of Google

It's not uncommon for sales reps to have a certain level of skepticism related to AI. Even if data backs up a recommendation, reps may not be certain if it is trustworthy. But AI is not a pie-in-the-sky concept. It's likely part of your everyday life already. Each time you order an Uber, browse suggested items on Amazon, or select a show on Netflix, you are trusting AI. It helps you make decisions and save time in your personal life. Why not harness its power to help you be a more productive and profitable salesperson?

Salespeople who embrace technology and put it into practice will have a competitive advantage. Those who do not will quickly be left behind or made obsolete when their competition starts using AI.

According to recent research by Salesforce, high-performing sales teams are almost five times more likely to be using AI than underperforming teams. Salesforce also stated that sales leaders expect AI adoption to grow faster than any other technology, and for good reason. McKinsey analysts writing in Harvard Business Review estimate that AI can create $1.4 to $2.6 trillion of value in marketing and sales.[10]

"Sales performance management tools have proliferated (more than 7,000 sales and marketing software applications by one recent count) to the point at which sales organizations struggle to separate the hype from proven value...On the flip side, some sales organizations that are skeptical of new tools miss the opportunity to deploy their sales teams more efficiently at higher-quality prospects."

- Bain

Further, a Bain survey found that high-growth companies have more effective data and analytics capabilities and deploy 25% more digital tools with wider adoption than low-growth companies. The results tell us that successful sales efforts rely on acceptance, application, and mastery of technology. Leading sales organizations of tomorrow will move beyond using technology to track selling and pipeline activity to reduce the administrative burden and empower sales reps to sell more effectively.

APPLICATIONS FOR AI IN SALES

"There's a lot of automation that can happen that isn't a replacement of humans, but of mind-numbing behavior."

- Stewart Butterfield, CEO of Slack

McKinsey found that digital leaders in B2B sales achieve up to five times the revenue growth and up to eight times the earnings of their peers before interest and taxes, but only one in three

10. Michael Chui,Nicolaus Henke and Mehdi Miremadi. "Most of AI's Business Uses Will Be in Two Areas." Harvard Business Review, 24 July 2018, hbr.org/2018/07/most-of-ais-business-uses-will-be-in-two-areas.

companies has deployed digital solutions at scale. What should B2B sales leaders do to deploy digital solutions and maximize value generated? According to McKinsey, they should apply digital thinking to:

- Commercial Processes: Make sure your sales process and pricing are modernized and leverages digital tools.

- Customer Journey: Use digital tools to make the customer's journey as convenient as possible.

- Innovate for Tomorrow: Ask yourself, how can we grow beyond our core business to evolve as technology evolves?

Essentially, to use digital tools to maximize your growth potential, think about where your money comes from today, where it will (or could) come from in the future, and how well are you using digital tools to bridge the gap.

Sales organizations are beginning to apply AI in a variety of areas ranging from administrative applications to sales forecasting and messaging.

ADMINISTRATIVE TASKS

Perhaps the most obvious application of AI is its ability to power administrative items such as automatic emails, notes, and activity logging, just to name a few. These are the most straightforward tasks to automate to free up more time to prepare for meetings and interact with top-priority prospects.

DEAL EVALUATION

As we have mentioned in other portions of this book, a great deal of time and resources goes into pursuing a deal before it is closed. A crucial trait that sets great performers apart from average ones is knowing the difference between a deal that is a good fit for your company and one that is not worth pursuing at all. AI can classify what your best customers and deals look like and recommend whether to pursue a deal or not based on previous successes and failures.

PROSPECTING

Like deal evaluation, AI can help you with lead scoring (prioritizing your viable leads). Beyond that, it can help you decide how and when to reach out to a prospect and when to discount. AI identifies patterns in deals that are most likely to be converted based on information such as engagement with marketing materials, titles, geography, company size, and more. Beyond helping you decide who to contact and when, it can also help you contact them. That can be through a targeted email or through robotic dialing that only passes calls through to you if they connect.

FORECASTING

In the past, a fair amount of pressure was placed on sales leaders to make accurate sales projections. Without AI, this process comes with a steep learning curve. Today, AI helps sales leaders get a realistic outlook on the quarter ahead based on previous performance.

MESSAGING

AI also has the power to not only identify who you should contact, but also what you should say to them. You can leverage AI to identify upselling and cross-selling opportunities and craft customer-centric emails and ad campaigns. And products like Chorus.ai compile a great deal on the total interaction (voice. email, marketing and other)we have with our prospects and clients and leverages AI to ensure we learn from our selling successes and failures alike.

LEVERAGE TECH TO BE MORE PRODUCTIVE AND PROFITABLE BUT DO SO WITH THE HUMAN TOUCH

"Whether it's GE, Amazon or Uber, they are all succeeding because they recognized that we now live in a digital world, and in this new world, customers are different. The way people buy has changed for good. We have new expectations as consumers. We prefer outcomes over ownership. We prefer customization, not standardization. And we want constant improvement, not planned obsolescence. We want a new way to engage with business. We want services, not products. The one-size-fits-all approach isn't going to cut it anymore. And to succeed in this new digital world, companies have to transform."

- Tien Tzuo, Subscribed: Why the Subscription Model Will Be Your Company's Future - and What to Do About It

When you engage AI to reduce mundane tasks, you will have more time to focus on more meaningful work. Not only that, you will have the ability to improve sales outreach without adding to your team. However, technology is only as effective as the human implementing it is thoughtful.

We have more opportunity to scale and connect than ever before, but the technology we use does not remove all need for effort and thought. AI can be leveraged to create ineffective SPAM as much as it can be used to generate ingeniously targeted campaigns. The difference lies in how you choose to use it.

The reality is the importance of preparation, a strong value proposition, and a meaningful relationship hasn't gone away. Technology—when used intelligently—just gets us there faster. Make technology your servant!

CHAPTER TAKEAWAYS

MAKE TECHNOLOGY YOUR SERVANT

Why not harness the power of technology to help you be a more productive and profitable salesperson? Salespeople who embrace technology and put it into practice will have a competitive advantage. Those who do not will quickly be left behind or made obsolete when their competition starts using AI.

APPLICATIONS FOR AI IN SALES:

- Automate Administrative Tasks: Set up automatic emails, notes, and activity logging to free up more time to prepare for meetings and interact with top-priority prospects.

- Evaluate Deals: Use AI to classify what your best customers and deals look like and evaluate whether to pursue a deal or not based on your previous successes and failures.

- Prospect: Set up lead scoring to prioritize your leads, identify patterns in deals that are most likely to be converted, and plan your outreach based on your CRM's insights.

- Forecast: Use digital tools to make realistic projections based on previous performance.

- Craft your Messaging: Leverage AI to identify upselling and cross-selling opportunities and craft customer-centric email and ad campaigns.

CLOUD TITAN:
ANTHONY FERNICOLA,
SALESFORCE, PRESIDENT,
CHIEF CUSTOMER OFFICER

A 35+ year Enterprise Software Sales Leader Positioned to Lead in the Mobile Cloud Computing Environment

ABOUT ANTHONY

Anthony "Tony" Fernicola has been a top sales leader in the software industry for 35+ years. He is known for his ability to build high-performing teams that deliver customer success. He began his career at Unisys. Unisys was the first company to bring to market a commercially viable computer system. Fernicola spent 16 years there in various leadership roles in sales and product management servicing the financial services industry. After Unisys, Fernicola served as Senior Vice President at Oracle for 17 years. At Oracle, he grew their North America Technology Organization into one of the company's largest revenue-generating business groups. He also served in various other leadership roles at Oracle and became known for leading key transformational initiatives. Today, Fernicola is President, Chief Customer Officer at Salesforce, by far the largest cloud application software company on the planet. He holds an MBA in Computer Science and a Bachelor of Science (B.S.) in Marketing and Economics from Manhattan College.

The most powerful theme in Anthony Fernicola's career is innovation. He has successfully navigated several draconic technology changes throughout his tenure. During his career, Fernicola has faced major swings in technology and sales philosophies. In 1995, when he joined Oracle, the company was on a steep upward trajectory led by its charismatic and fiercely growth focused leader, Larry Ellison. The world of hardware, application, and technology sales was transforming rapidly. After 17 years of enormous success and intense learning at Oracle, he was recruited over to Salesforce as President,Global Enterprise Sales to lead the enterprise software sales team worldwide.

At both Unisys and Oracle, he became adept at running large and complex sales operations on a spreadsheet. He quickly learned that as a worldwide sales executive at a hyper-growth company like Salesforce, he needed much more powerful and precise tools to manage the business. Fortunately those were the exact tools that Salesforce had developed and were selling into the marketplace. Tony for the first time had state of the art software in which to manage his sales organization and customer relationships

One of his responsibilities was giving the enterprise sales forecast at the executive committee meeting each Monday. He was responsible for sharing the large deals, where they were in the process, and the next steps to get the deals closed. Preparing for this meeting each week was a hugely stressful endeavor. The information had to be precise, fully inclusive, and as close to real time as possible.

The tech world and Salesforce in particular seized the opportunity to help sales leaders like Fernicola prepare for meetings like that Monday morning meeting. When Fernicola came over to Salesforce, their Salesforce1 mobile app revolutionized the way he stayed connected to his teams on a 24/7 basis. Having access to sales and customer data on the phone allowed salespeople, who are never sitting still but are always in motion traveling and making calls, to make updates throughout the day. Second, it revolutionized the way he forecasted and conducted pipeline reviews. As a sales leader he was able to set up alerts so he could see when a deal probability changed in any way.

However, there is no silver bullet in sales. The innovation continues every day. A few years after Salesforce1 was released, the complementary Einstein Analytics product was introduced to the market. Einstein Analytics, transformed his ability to view year-over-year revenue, product, geographic, selling capacity, and attrition numbers. Within a year or so of joining Salesforce, Fernicola was able to pull all the data he once had to call his analyst for, now completely on his own right from his cell phone whenever he needed it. This greatly reduced his stress level and markedly increased the selling productivity of himself and his team.

Continuing to innovate Einstein AI was released a few years later. This introduced machine learning into the sales process in ways that could never have been imagined . Utilizing Einstein AI capabilities along with Analytics and the mobile app Fernicola was now able to use the technology in three essential ways daily to enhance the overall sales operation.

1. Prediction: The Einstein AI app runs algorithms based on current data and history to predict your sales forecast. It is just a prediction, but with the right data in the system, it has proved highly accurate.

2. Deal Rating: Based on current and historic data, Einstein AI gives each deal a rating regarding how strong or weak the deal appears to be based on historic deal measures and the likelihood of closure

3. Tasks: Einstein will look at each opportunity and let you know if a task is overdue or the size of the deal seems to be outside the norm with the buying pattern of the company amongst many other indicators that provide deal guidance

Fernicola could never ever go back to running a sales organization using spreadsheets where information is outdated the minute you pull or print the report. Well-designed mobile sales applications along with artificial intelligence help facilitate and streamline the entire decision-making process. It makes us more efficient, effective, and as commission sales reps and leaders provides an opportunity to earn much more.

However, with all the power of harnessed technology, Fernicola remains a true relationship-focused sales executive. Technology is augmenting the way we sell; however, it will never replace the power of human connection. At the end of the day, people are still buying from people. Yes, a lot has changed. Yes, the process might be a bit less personal than the early days, but a lot remains the same. Intelligent technology helps us ensure we are focusing on the right relationships at the exact right times and that ensures more productivity and more selling success.

TITAN TIPS:

- Never ask anyone to do anything you wouldn't do yourself. A major component of being a strong leader is the willingness to get in the trenches and lead from the front.

- Relationships count; make them real and personal if possible. Not all relationships are created equal. Build real relationships by reaching out, not to sell something or because you need something but to just connect and show you care. Don't be afraid to be vulnerable or to get personal. For example, always involve spouses or significant others at events or dinners when appropriate.

- Remember, you cannot look smart with bad numbers. No matter what impressive narrative you spin, numbers speak for themselves. Focus on doing the right things for the right reasons and results will follow.

COVID-19 SPARKS DIGITAL SALES TRANSFORMATION

"We've seen two years' worth of digital transformation in two months. From remote teamwork and learning, to sales and customer service, to critical cloud infrastructure and security— we are working alongside customers every day to help them adapt and stay open for business in a world of remote everything."Satya Nadella, CEO of Microsoft, April of 2020,

Satya is correct, COVID-19 has been an incredible catalyst for transformation. At the time of press, we are about 6 months into the COVID-19 crisis and the implications of COVID-19 have not slowed us down one bit.

SaaS companies large and small have seized this opportunity to rethink their go-to-market models across the board. The availability and adoption of technology and work-from-home culture asks not "When will we go back to the office?" but rather, "Will we go back to the office?"

It is safe to say we will never go back to the way it was, at least not exactly. However, there will always be cases where face-to-face selling will remain more productive and/or absolutely necessary.

Interestingly, as our American Airlines AAdvantage accounts will attest, we haven't traveled much the past few months, but our selling performance and productivity has actually increased notably.

In Mark's case, he attributes this increase to more meetings (albeit virtual) with executives. The more meetings he and his team have with senior executives each week, the more business they sign up and deliver. No matter how efficient he felt he was scheduling flights and booking up his schedule, no human salesperson can out-perform the efficiency of Zoom.

This approach may not always be sustainable. We, like many of you, are certainly feeling a bit of video conference fatigue. Nonetheless, we would all do well to embrace this adaptation. Maybe it is time to invest in more at-home office equipment. Mark's response to the home office lockup was to add a killer DTEN 55 inch Zoom Room Device where he can walk around and use a virtual whiteboard while presenting, instead of sitting at his desk for 12 hours straight, clicking from one Zoom meeting to the next.

In this post COVID-19 "new normal" we find ourselves in, we believe there is an unprecedented opportunity to significantly lower the cost of selling, while notably increasing consistent achievement of revenue goals. The key is adapting with the world rather than letting it leave you behind.

Fortunately, we have had the opportunity to work with thought leaders who study the effect of technology on sales. Most notably, Joel LeBon, Professor at Johns Hopkins University Carey Business School and Executive Director of the Science of Digital Business Development Initiative. For many years before COVID-19, Joel was studying the effect of increasingly powerful technology on sales and marketing methods. His work has proven time-and-time-again that by fully leveraging people, process, and technology to build world-class business development innovation centers, companies can drive revenue at an unprecedented level of reliability and efficiency.

Now that truly virtual sales teams are the new normal, we are learning even more about how to deliver this virtual salesforce as a service in ways that far outpace brick-and-mortar, traditional sales approaches.

Now to be clear, this isn't for every industry or every market segment, but it fits in some way in almost all go-to-market strategies. Virtual salesforce success starts with a hyper-segmentation of your target market, well thought-out sales technology design and integration, and exceptional training for the inside and/or virtual selling representatives. The rest is virtual selling history.

#12 | SALES AND LEADERSHIP THROUGH CRISIS

We have led sales teams through three significant global crises that hugely impacted businesses: the 2000 Dot.com crash, the 2001 Terror Attacks (9/11), and the 2008 Financial Crisis (Great Recession). Now, we are facing another crisis: COVID-19. Every crisis presents different challenges and uniquely impacts different sections of the market. During the COVID-19 crisis, salespeople have had to pivot in a whole new way. This crisis has an unprecedented global scale. However, it bears some of the same hallmarks as other crises when it comes to determining what to do next as a sales professional.

During 9/11, Mark was running a group of consulting sales leaders at Oracle that needed to figure out how to figure out a way to grow after this devastating tragedy. The team went from fast growth to the bottom dropping out after 9/11 occurred.

Mark was asked to support the team by moving from leading a successful sales team to temporarily becoming what could only be called a "hatchet man". He was asked to help out by handling the face-to-face layoffs within Oracle's consulting group throughout different parts of the country. It was the worst part of his career. He was a young professional who had to inform individuals that were much older, had children in college and other major financial commitments, that they no longer had a job.

In difficult times, if you are a leader, you are called to become a psychologist. Having a strong leader in place to mentor the team left behind is vitally important. Fortunately, a crisis is rarely permanent. People learn, people pivot, and people move on and thrive beyond crisis. They do so much faster when they have a strong leader to set the tone.

In this chapter, we dive into our top suggestions for forging through any crisis.

ASK YOURSELF, WHAT DO I NEED TO DO FOR THE COMPANY TO SURVIVE?

First assess the damage likely inflicted, both short-term and long-term. Get down to essentials. Look at your current resources and consider this potential reality: what would we do if no new money came in for 18 months? This usually means making difficult decisions. However, making cuts and being conservative in times of crisis is often what puts you in a position to be able to execute on your long-term strategy. In fact, being efficient with your resources in times good and bad, will make you stronger when challenges do arise. The companies that have preserved liquidity and have planned for challenges, do exceptionally well during crises.

SCALE DOWN, INTELLIGENTLY

A time of crisis is a great time to retune yourself with other parts of your business. In high times, we get tunnel vision, and can overlook the realities of operations. Connect with team members from other parts of your business. Ensure your new go-to-market strategy is executable. Think beyond top-line revenue. This is the time to get more involved with product marketing than ever before. Stabilize your spending in every way possible, but don't decrease staff unless it becomes a true matter of solvency. Your people are the lifeblood of your company and don't lower that power unless entirely forced to do so.

KNOW THAT YOU CAN'T SLAP A BAND-AID ON WEAK CULTURE

Difficult times separate true leaders from those just going through the motions. Challenges spotlight company culture, or lack thereof. When all the boats are floating, a company can get away with a weak culture or leader, but as soon as the tide goes out, if the leaders and culture are not strong, you are going to struggle in a big way.

LEAN INTO LEADERSHIP

When things are hard, people look to their leaders more than ever. You want leaders who have a wartime mentality strong enough to lead the team into battle. Many younger professionals today have never seen a recession, they especially need leaders who can share with them how to navigate the challenge, evolve, and retain focus. Great leaders connect with their employees on a personal level and think about the lifestyle impact their employees are experiencing.

LOOK FOR THE OPPORTUNITIES

If you are fortunate to work for a capital-efficient company, you are able to take advantage of a crisis and gain market share where other companies have been capitally inefficient. Like Warren Buffet has often stated, "be fearful when others are greedy and greedy when others are fearful". Look for silver linings and opportunities. Carefully watch the green shoots and move faster than your competitors, but not so fast that you are exposed. We need to be exceptionally compassionate to people, but don't have any such responsibilities to our competitive corporations. If your company doubles in size, you will have the capacity to hire many of the employees that your competitor will have to lay off.

FOCUS ON HUMANITY FIRST

This is always important, but especially in times of crisis. Tone down your sales messaging and focus on the human being you are interacting with and serving. Share appropriately what you and the company are doing to help and find out from your clients and prospects what you can do for them. Show patience and empathy to your people. You never know what someone is dealing with financially and/or emotionally.

If you read the above list of suggestions for selling in crisis, you will see that many of the fundamental strategies we suggest to navigate the crisis are also the same things that will make you successful in sales in general.

CLOUD TITAN:
JIM STEELE, PRESIDENT, GLOBAL
STRATEGIC CUSTOMERS, SALESFORCE

Thrive through Crisis by Looking for the Opportunities

ABOUT JIM

For more than 35 years, Jim Steele has served as a cutting-edge technology sales leader. He began his career at IBM and went on to serve in senior sales leadership roles at leading cloud software organizations such as Ariba, Salesforce, and InsideSales.com. Throughout his career he has repeatedly been tasked with turning around difficult situations in the face of crisis. Today Jim serves as President of Global Strategic Customers at Salesforce. Prior to joining Salesforce, Jim served as Yext's Chief Revenue Officer and President at InsideSales.com. Prior to InsideSales.com Jim was Chief Customer Officer and President of Worldwide Sales and Operations at Salesforce. During his 12-year tenure at Salesforce, Jim helped grow the company from $25 million to more than

$5 billion in revenue. He holds a B.S. in Civil Engineering from Bucknell University. He has been at the helm at some of the most successful SaaS sales engines that have ever been created.

Crisis is no stranger to Jim Steele. In fact, it's been a solid through line in his career. He came of age in the time of the Cold War, draft numbers, and the JFK assassination. During his 35+ year career as a sales leader he's navigated recessions, corporate downsizing, earthquakes, 9/11, and most recently-- a global pandemic. Through each crisis, he and his team have emerged stronger on the other side because of Jim's commitment to put people first, look for opportunities to help during a crisis, and to keep a positive attitude in the midst of change.

Jim's first true crisis was in 1987, about 8-9 years into his tenure at IBM. He had just taken the reins at the NYC/financial services branch office. It was his first bonafide management job. Just as he was transitioning over to that role, the infamous Black Monday rocked Wall Street. The Dow in one day fell 22.6% which would equate to over a 6,000 point drop from where the stock market was in early summer 2020.

No matter the carnage Jim walked into, he was tasked with selling to those very banks whose business models were torn to shreds by the biggest market disruption since the Great Depression.. These were dark times. Financial district employees were literally and sadly jumping from buildings.

Jim's new office was 300th out of 300 in IBM branch performance. His branch was the lowest in the nation due to poor employee attrition rates and financial performance. It would have been easy to be beaten down by this. Instead, Jim saw it as the best opportunity of his career: he had the opportunity to go from worst to first. He brought a fresh mindset to the branch and resized their strategy to serve customers, even though many of them were filing for bankruptcy. Within a year, Jim was branch manager of the year for IBM in the US.

In 1991, Jim was chosen to be assistant to the CIO at IBM. Despite the success at his branch, IBM was suffering financially. During 1991-1993 IBM's revenues decreased by 18 billion dollars and went from being one of the most respected businesses on the planet, to the laughing stock of the industry. They had no choice but to downsize.

As assistant to the CEO, Jim received calls daily from investors, shareholders, employees, and customers complaining that IBM was not delivering on their promises. Jim could see clearly that IBM needed to think outside of the box and that bureaucracy was standing in the way of their ability to innovate to better serve customers.

Jim was promoted from assistant to the CEO to lead sales in Southern California. Within a few weeks, the CEO he served was fired and the new CEO, Lou Gerstner rounded the troops and gave employees a reality check. The reality was that their customers, employees, and investors were extremely unhappy. IBM had lost the respect of the business community and over $5B in losses in 1992 (the highest loss ever by a company at that time).If they wanted to save the company they needed to think and act differently. He asked employees that were not willing to think differently to self select out and leave the company or be let go within 6-9 months.

IBM had the opportunity to prove itself and improve its reputation during a crisis in 1994. In January 1994, LA experienced a 7.8 earthquake and IBM's data center there was literally on fire. IBM engineers put the fire out and saved the city of LA from losing all of its records. During the earthquake many IBM customers were injured or killed. IBM immediately deployed a crisis management team to restore data to the centers for the next 6 months. All customers who were considering leaving IBM came back and were loyal because they saw how IBM responded to and supported them during the crisis. The mayor of LA presented the key to the city to IBM for their efforts. In addition, IBM reinforced its connection with their employee base,because of the way they supported them during the crisis. This is how long-term business goodwill is built.

After navigating these challenges, Jim knew that whenever a new low arose, there was an opportunity to come back stronger. When he moved to Asia for IBM in 1996, Asia soon after faced a devastating financial crisis as banks in the Philippines, Thailand, and Vietnam went belly up. He applied the lessons he learned during other challenging times that by focusing on helping people, keeping a positive attitude and an open mind, you can do well by doing good. He learned that if you act helpless in the face of crisis, you'll be helpless. If you take ownership of what you can control, you'll contribute to positive change.

Unfortunately, Jim's interactions with crises did not end after his time at IBM. He was working at Ariba in New York on 9/11. This time he was extremely proud of his company's response. Keith Krach the CEO of Ariba and now Under Secretary of our nation's Treasury Department made sure that Ariba's leaders focused first and foremost on taking care of people. Shortly after September 2001, after Ariba's meteoric rise during the fall of 2001 and the summer of 2002, the dot.com bust hit. Ariba dropped from $40 billion in market cap to $400 million and went from 3,000 people and growing to less than 700 people in 7 months.

Even in the face of that downfall, Jim knew that focusing on taking care of people is what would help him and his team emerge stronger on the other side. So, he prioritized going out on the road and thanking customers. He toured NYC shortly after 9/11 to simply check in and see if customers were safe and to share experiences together. He was not selling anything but empathy and it reflected positively on the business.

In 2002, Jim joined Salesforce. Funnily enough, because of the dot com bust, many said it was foolish to join an internet-focused company. With the advantage of hindsight, we of course now know that it was not foolish, but pure genius. Even in the face of skepticism about internet businesses, Salesforce was successful because they established themselves as a utility for delivering value quickly.

In 2007, Jim faced his second Wall Street financial melt down. Jim did what he always did: look for the opportunity to help in the face of crisis. Since everyone was struggling and going out of business, Jim knew that Salesforce could save them money because it was as effective or more and a fraction of the cost of competitors like SAP and Oracle. Jim showed his customers and prospects how a new model could benefit them while his competitors bemoaned their fate.

During any crisis, companies with the right mindset will survive and thrive. Yext, Jim's current employer helps companies and customers get direct answers to questions. In the face of COVID-19, they adopted the philosophy Jim always employs during crisis: focus on taking care of people and look for the opportunity to help. Yext acted quickly to reach out to their customers to see how they could support them, ensured employees were safe, and built a robust information hub that served as a source of truth containing answers to all COVID-19 related questions.

He realized that Yext was in a perfect position to help governments struggling to convey information to their scared and frustrated citizens. So he reached out to the CDC, State Department, and multiple states and offered Yext's product for free. They accepted and Yext's technology is helping the U.S. and the world manage the information necessary to keep us all as safe as possible. These types of gracious business acts build a company's reputation and reaffirms to its employees that they are part of something important and special..

Many people instinctively shut down in crisis. But the reality is: you have two choices. You can think about a crisis as all downside, or you can try to find the upside and the opportunity. And, as Jim has learned through every one of the numerous challenges and crises he's navigated throughout his career, putting people first, looking for the opportunity to help, and keeping a positive attitude has consistently delivered more positive results than dwelling on the negative side.

TITAN TIPS:

- Never take your customers for granted. Have a maniacal obsession with customer success. Interact with your customers in a way that is confident and passionate, not arrogant and cocky. And always think of your relationships with your customers as a journey, not a transaction.

- Think big. Consider this: What are 2-3 big targets you can shoot for that will change your career trajectory? Take action every day to move in the direction of those targets.

- LVI. Listen, Validate and Inspire. This is the formula for sales success. Tell stories, don't sell, be genuine, and establish an emotional connection with your customers.

- Embrace change. Always keep your beginners mindset and don't be afraid to reinvent yourself.

POSTSCRIPT

Like anything worth achieving in life, hard-won lessons are par for the course along the way. We hope that even the most analytical of you have learned from this book that "the soft stuff" is the stuff that moves the needle. Passion, velocity, grit, empathy, authenticity, creativity, resilience, trustworthiness, and innovative thinking are truly what set the top performers apart. We hope this book helps demystify the fundamentals of enterprise software sales success.

It is easy to get overwhelmed in this industry. The ecosystem evolves. Technology changes every day. Clients are demanding more and more from us. Competition is fierce. Sales are more and more complex. But, even when you face the most complex of deals— when you are partnering with another company and selling with multiple executives at more than five companies that all have a vested interest and influence on your sale—remember that success boils down to the ability to connect on a human level.

Listen. Show up consistently. Do good work. Be honest. Learn from your mistakes. These simple things are truly the bread and butter of success in our space.

Remember, it has to start with your own WHY and your passion in life must align with all the great things you get to do every day as a cloud seller. If it doesn't, nothing we share in this book will serve you.

But if it does, you have set yourself up for an amazing career where your efforts will impact the enterprise value of your clients, which will drive more jobs and offer financial security to their employees and other stakeholders. You won't get to save lives in a hospital or design and engineer a robot that can enter a burning building and save lives. However, you will get to be an important enabler to the companies or governmental entities that do achieve those things,

Thank you for allowing us to take you on this journey and share the stories of some of the most exceptional business executives of our generation. We are proud to be a very small part of the impact software and SaaS has had on the world economy and we hope we have shared some ideas and prescriptions that help you in your career and life.

All the best!

- Mark and Paul

ACKNOWLEDGMENTS

First and foremost, we are incredibly grateful for all the blessings that have been bestowed upon us. The most valuable of those blessings is the love and support of our amazing families and friends. We only hope we can give back a fraction of what you give us every day.

Our success and happiness were nearly assured by the untiring efforts and sacrifices made by our second-generation parents, Paul and Elaine Melchiorre and Charles and Margaret Petruzzi. The excellent foundation they built for us was doubly bolstered by the support of the exceptional mentors and business partners we have had the immense pleasure and honor to work with.

There are no words to describe our love and devotion to our families. Supporting them has been our driving motivation throughout our careers. We are incredibly grateful to have amazing wives that hold our families together and are the real CEOs of the Petruzzi and Melchiorre households.

Our most precious blessings include the honor of being the fathers of the most thoughtful, caring, giving, empathetic, passionate, determined, and intelligent children anyone could hope for. Special thanks to Paul's children, Kristen, Paolo, Alexis, and Graziella, and to Mark's, Max and Mirabella.

The book came together thanks to the expertise of many talented veterans of the software sales industry. We are endlessly grateful for the network of trusted colleagues, family, and friends who made this piece the resource it is. Thank you to our brilliant and inspiring titans Gerhard Gschwandtner, Jeff Laue, Joe Fuca, Cathy Minter, Jim Steele, Maria Martinez, Bill Campbell, Eileen Voynick, Greg Holmes, Charlie Green, Klaus Besier, Myron Radio, Marc Benioff, Todd Beamer, and Tony Fernicola.

In addition to our featured Cloud Titans, we thank Keith Krach, Joe Dibartolomao, Bob Calderoni, Ben Pastro, Gabe Cavacchioli, Paul Wahl, Matt Radman, Marcel Florez, Shannon Copeland, Joe Canariato, Gary Fedor, Paul Nix, Wendy Gaskill, Michael Coates, Michael Noel, Melissa Swartz, Andrew Fritts, Jim Jensen, Al Ingrassia, Greg Swick, Ken Fox, Mike Noel, Dan Hynes, Mark Roberge, Kristie Ornelas, Ted Malley, Eddie Birchfield, Sirisha Chandraraju, Glen Hughes, Michael Coates, Wendy Gaskill, Dave Orrico, Monje Llorente, Warren Wirth, Ivan Nikkhoo, Maria Floria, Mike Crawford, Peter Szary, Al Turovlin, Alan Rudolph, Don Lynch, and many others that our editor tells us just can't be fit in. We apologize in advance for any omissions.

Special thanks to Laurel Sutherland for her tireless work supporting us on this endeavor. Her professionalism and positive attitude, combined with her exceptional writing and research skills, made working with her an absolute pleasure. This book would not be what it is today without her support. Many thanks to the other top-notch production resources who helped make this book a reality, including Liz Borchert, who designed the cover and layout of this publication.

CPSIA information can be obtained
at www.ICGtesting.com
Printed in the USA
BVHW070514230221
600782BV00004B/244